BLAST OFF!

on
Ohio Reading
Level 5
Second Edition

This book belongs to: _____

Helping the schoolhouse meet the
standards of the statehouse™

Buckle Down
PUBLISHING COMPANY

Acknowledgments

Excerpt from "Young Ladies Don't Slay Dragons" by Joyce Hovelsrud copyright © 1974 by Rand McNally & Company, renewed © 2002 by Joyce Hovelsrud Rodell. Reprinted by permission of the author.

Excerpt from *Anne of Green Gables* by Lucy Maud Montgomery, adapted by Mike Acton.

Excerpt from *Don Quixote* by Miguel de Cervantes Saavedra, adapted by Gordon Mertz.

Excerpt reprinted with the permission of Simon & Schuster Books for Young Readers, an imprint of Simon & Schuster Children's Publishing Division, from *I Left My Sneakers In Dimension X* by Bruce Coville. Copyright © 1994 by Bruce Coville.

Excerpt from "Going Too Far" by Mildred Howells. Public domain.

Excerpt from "A Very Little Sphinx" from *Poems Selected For Young People* by Edna St. Vincent Millay. Public domain.

Excerpt from "Dismasted!" by Frank Robben. Copyright © 1996 by Frank Robben. Reprinted by permission of the author.

"Peter Cooper's Tom Thumb" photograph from the Bureau of Public Roads, Department of Commerce, reprinted courtesy of the Library of Congress, Prints and Photographs Division, LC-USZ62-98456.

Excerpt from "The First American Locomotive," from *Personal Recollections of the Baltimore & Ohio Railroad* by John Hazlehurst Boneval Latrobe, adapted by Julia Render.

Willie Nelson performs at Farm Aid 2001 on September 29, 2001, in Noblesville, Indiana. Photograph copyright © 2001 by Ebet Roberts, reprinted courtesy of Farm Aid.

Excerpt from "To Build a Fire" from *Lost Face* by Jack London. Public domain.

VIKING 2 image of Mars Utopian Plain reprinted courtesy of NASA Jet Propulsion Laboratory, image number PIA01522.

Excerpt from *The War of the Worlds* by H. G. Wells, adapted by Alan Noble.

"View of Earth, showing Africa, Europe and Asia taken by APOLLO 11 crewmember." Reprinted courtesy of the National Aeronautics and Space Administration, NASA photo ID number AS11-36-5355.

Ohio Academic Content Standards for English Language Arts and Ohio Proficiency Learning Outcomes for Reading were developed by the Ohio Department of Education.

Every effort has been made by the publisher to locate each owner of the copyrighted material reprinted in this publication and to secure the necessary permissions. If there are any questions regarding the use of these materials, the publisher will take appropriate corrective measures to acknowledge ownership in future publications.

ISBN 0-7836-2886-2

Catalog #BF OH5R 1   2 3 4 5 6 7 8 9 10

President and Publisher: Douglas J. Paul, Ph.D.; Editorial Director: John Hansen; Project Editor: Doria Knebel; Editor: Mike Acton; Production Editor: Michael Hankes; Production Director: Jennifer Booth; Production Supervisor: Ginny York; Art Director: Chris Wolf; Graphic Designer: Tumara L. Wilcox.

Cover image: © Corbis

TABLE OF CONTENTS

Introduction

Blast Off on Ohio Reading, Level 5, is about to take you on a journey through the skills you'll need to do well on reading tests. We'll show you what to expect on these types of tests, including the kinds of passages and questions you are likely to see. We'll also give you tips to help answer all kinds of questions.

Along the way, you'll review basic reading skills. This will help you not only on tests but also in the reading you do just for fun. By the end of our journey, you might even think of reading tests as a way to show off your skills.

Ready? Let's go!

A Reader Training Program

Astronauts don't just wake up one morning, hop into a space shuttle, and take a spin around the planet. They go through a training program. They learn to move in the weightlessness of space. They learn to operate the spacecraft. And they learn how to perform neat experiments in space. This all takes lots and lots of practice.

Think of this book as a training program for taking reading tests. The key to a successful reading training program—just like the key to a successful astronaut training program—is practice. The more you read, the better you'll read.

If you train with this book, you will learn a few new skills and brush up on some old ones. You can make great leaps in your reading ability with just a little bit of practice on your own.

This doesn't mean you have to lock yourself in your room day after day, reading stacks and stacks of books, cut off from your family and friends, suffering from thirst and starvation. Books aren't the only reading material out there. Just look around you. Words are everywhere!

Here are some ideas for practicing your reading. Check the ones you think you might read this week.

✍

❏ the back of a cereal box

❏ instructions to your favorite video or board game

❏ comic books or comic strips in a newspaper

❏ booklets that come with a compact disc (CD)

❏ directions for using or putting together a toy

❏ sports trading cards

❏ recipes

❏ descriptions of television shows in *TV Guide* or your local newspaper

❏ your school newsletter

❏ magazines such as *American Girl* or *Sports Illustrated for Kids*

Can you think of others? Write your ideas on the following lines.

_____

_____

_____

Testwise Strategies™ for Taking Reading Tests

Doing your best on reading tests will depend a lot on your reading skills. But it will also depend on three other things:

- Knowing what to expect on these types of tests
- Knowing strategies for answering test questions
- Knowing that you have practiced your skills

This book will help you with all three. Let's begin by cruising through the basic tips for taking any kind of reading test.

Tip 1 **Read the entire passage.**

Read through each passage from beginning to end before going on to the questions. This will help you find the **main idea**—what the passage is mostly about. You don't have to memorize every detail as you go. Just focus on getting the big picture.

You may want to stop and go over a difficult idea to make sure you understand it. That's okay. Just be careful not to get stuck. Keep moving until you come to the end of the passage.

Tip 2 **Learn about common question types.**

Certain types of questions often appear on reading tests. For example, some questions may ask about the main idea of a passage. Others may ask about supporting details. Learning about the different question types will help you know what to expect on test day. At each stop on our journey, we will teach you about one of these question types. We'll also give you tips on how to answer each type of question.

Tip 3 **Read the questions carefully.**

Read each question slowly and carefully. Make sure you understand what the question is asking. And don't jump ahead to pick an answer before you've read _all_ the answer choices. The first choice may look good, but the last choice may look even better.

Tip 4 **Answer every question, even if you have to guess.**

If you aren't sure of the answer, give it your best guess. Before guessing, cross out any choices that seem wrong.

But what if you're completely clueless? A blind guess is better than no guess at all. If you don't answer a question, you can't possibly get it right.

Tip 5 **Base your answers on information from the passage.**

A reading test is used to find out how well you read. It is not trying to find out how much you know about the topic of the passage. Always remember to base your answers on information from the passage.

Tip 6 **For written responses, answer all parts of the question and support your answer with ideas from the passage.**

On many reading tests (and throughout this book), you'll be asked to write out your answer for some questions. Make sure to answer each part of the question. It's also important that you give specific reasons for your answer. Your reasons should come from the passage. Use as many details as you can from the passage, but write them in your own words.

Tip 7 **Use your best handwriting.**

Some of these written-response questions will ask you to write only a few words or sentences. Others will ask you to write a longer, more thoughtful response.

You may write in cursive or you may print. It's okay to cross out or erase things you have written; just be sure that your answer is neat enough for others to read.

Tip 8 **Relax, and have fun!**

Just as astronauts train for a shuttle mission, you are "in training" for taking reading tests. After working through this book, you will have the skills needed to do your best. When the time comes, you'll be ready.

So on test day, sit back, relax, and have fun. By then, your reading skills will be *out of this world!*

Getting Started

Getting ready for a reading test is a little like cleaning your room. It requires work. Yet, it's also filled with interesting surprises. Reading a good story can be as exciting as finding that peanut butter sandwich you thought was lost forever. And learning new tips to help you on a test can be as satisfying as having a clean room.

If you're like most people, the toughest part of any job is getting started. Where do you begin? If you want to get the job done—and if you want to do it well—you'll need a plan.

A plan also helps when preparing for a reading test. In this unit, you'll start with the "big picture," finding out about main ideas and details. Then you'll learn some tips to help you figure out the meanings of unknown words. You will build on these important word skills as you work through the rest of the book. By the time you've finished the entire book, your reading skills will be as polished as the top of your freshly waxed dresser. And you'll know that you have the skills to do your best on any reading test.

In This Unit

- ◆ *What's the Big Idea?*
- ◆ *Details, Details, Details*
- ◆ *Be a Word Detective*
- ◆ *What's the Word?*

Lesson 1

What's the Big Idea?

"Hey, I saw a great movie last night."
"Oh, yeah? What was it about?"

When you tell a friend what a movie or television show is mostly about, you are telling the **main idea**. You can do this with reading, too.

Tip 1 **Many passages have one clear main idea.**

Sometimes a passage will come right out and tell you its main idea in one sentence.

> Squirrel Hollow is not a big town. In fact, it is so small, the Water Department is a hand pump in the town square. And the Squirrel Hollow Fire Department is made up of one bucket, a pair of rain boots, and a red 10-speed bicycle.

What is the main idea of this passage? You will find it in the first sentence: "Squirrel Hollow is not a big town." The rest of the passage gives details to support the main idea.

Now you try.

1. Read the following passage, then underline the sentence that tells the main idea.

> Juan stood with his left foot firmly planted on the third-base bag. He listened to the cheers. It was his fourth hit of the game. Two of them had been home runs. His hitting had been excellent, as usual, pushing the Bulldogs to an 8–3 lead over the Hornets. There could be no doubt: Juan was the best baseball player in the league.

Tip 2 **Sometimes you have to piece together important ideas that lead you to a main idea.**

The main idea won't always jump right out at you. Sometimes you'll need to figure it out on your own. Read the following passage from *Good-bye, My*

Wishing Star by Vicki Grove. Then write the main idea of the passage on the lines provided.

> I kind of floated through the rest of that day, aware that my neck was burning and that most of the reason for that was that Arthur was sitting three rows behind me in class. When it was finally time to go home, I didn't have the nerve to look over my shoulder at him, but when Marla and I were in our seat on the bus, I glanced in his direction, and he smiled at me.

2. What is the main idea of the passage?

_____

_____

Like fictional (made-up) stories, nonfiction passages also have a main idea, or possibly several important ideas that relate to a main topic. First, think about the topic (general subject) of the passage. Read the following passage, then answer Numbers 3 and 4.

> Have you ever smelled the sweet scent of a beeswax candle? Don't take it for granted, because bees worked a long time to make it! Worker bees develop special wax-producing glands once they are about ten days old. When the bees eat honey, these glands convert the sugar from the honey into wax. The wax oozes through the tiny pores on the bee's body, sort of like when you sweat. Then it forms flakes which the bee picks off its body and chews. Finally, the bee is ready to put the wax onto the honeycomb. Each bee makes wax for about six days of its life. Think of all the bees it takes to make one sweet-smelling beeswax candle!

3. What is the topic of the passage?
   A. pores
   B. honey
   C. glands
   D. beeswax

4. What is the main idea or ideas of the passage?

_____

_____

Tip 3 **Summarize the passage as you read.**

As you read, think about what you are reading. After reading a long paragraph or several short paragraphs, ask yourself, "What is this part of the passage *mostly* about?" **Summarizing** can help you make sure you understand the passage.

If part of the passage is really confusing to you, go back and reread it. But don't get hung up on minor details. As you read further along in the passage, the confusing part may become clear to you.

Practice Tip 3 as you read the following passage.

Anansi and His Dinner Guest

an Ashanti Folktale

retold by Auntie May-o

The sly spider named Anansi appears in many folktales from West Africa and Jamaica. The following story tells about one of Anansi's many adventures.

Gather 'round, children. I have to tell you another story about that trickster spider, Anansi. Listen carefully now, for Anansi's foolishness always teaches a lesson. Yes, children, he may be a foolish spider, but he teaches us about our own abilities to act like fools.

This time Anansi was in his web about to enjoy his supper. All of a sudden, who comes along but poor Turtle, tired from a day of wandering. Of course, Anansi invited Turtle in to share a meal, because that was the custom in Anansi's country and he could not ignore custom.

Turtle was so hungry that he reached out for something to eat. "Oh, no," said Anansi. "In this country, you must first wash before eating at a stranger's table. Didn't you know that? There's a stream at the bottom of the hill."

Turtle was very hungry, but he did as Anansi said by trudging down to the stream, where he cleaned up for supper. When he returned, the meal was half-finished, and Anansi was eating as fast as he could.

Again, Turtle reached out for something to eat. Again, Anansi stopped him. "Look at your dusty paws," said Anansi. "I thought you said you washed them."

"I did," groaned Turtle, "but the trail back from the stream was dusty." Turtle left to wash a second time.

This time, Turtle was careful to walk back on the grass. But when he returned, Anansi was wiping his mouth after having finished *all* of the food. "Delicious!" burped the spider.

"Thank you for taking me into your home," said the disappointed turtle. "If you should ever be in my neighborhood, please feel free to stop by and enjoy my company." And with that, the hungry turtle left for his home.

Sure enough, some time later Anansi happened to be stuck in Turtle's village, alone and tired from a long day of traveling. He decided to pay Turtle a visit.

"Welcome to my place," said Turtle. "Relax and make yourself at home while I prepare some dinner." With that, Turtle dived into the river.

After awhile, the hungry Anansi wondered what had happened to him. Just then, Turtle's head <u>emerged</u> from the water and announced, "Come down and join me. Dinner is served."

Anansi jumped into the water, but he was a spider, so light that he could only float. What could he do? He was hungry, and as the wise ones say, necessity is the mother of invention. So Anansi took some rocks he found by the riverside and put them into his jacket pockets. What do you know, those rocks helped Anansi sink down to Turtle's table.

Turtle was about to enjoy a most wonderful feast. He had a platter full of crabs, clams, oysters, shrimp, and seven kinds of fish, all perfectly prepared and ready to be eaten.

Anansi's mouth was watering. He reached out for something tasty, when Turtle said "Oh, no. In my country, a stranger must take off his jacket before he eats at another one's table. That is the custom of this land." Anansi had to follow custom, so he took off his coat, and what do you know, he floated to the water's surface. The last sounds he heard were of Turtle munching on that wonderful meal.

So you see, children, Anansi teaches us yet another lesson: Don't try to outwit somebody by being dishonest or cheating, because they may outwit you in the same manner. ❖

The Trickster

Tricksters appear in folktales from many cultures. The trickster is traditionally an animal that acts like a human. He tries to outwit others, or fate, by clever schemes. He might be the spider Anansi from West African tales, the coyote of North American Indian tradition, or the fox from both South American and Japanese stories. The trickster can also be seen in such modern-day characters as Daffy Duck and Bugs Bunny.

Often the trickster is a fool who thinks he can control his life. Sometimes he is a hero fooling others who are trying to destroy him. Whether a fool or a fooler, the trickster's role in storytelling around the world is to allow people to laugh at fate and see the humor in life.

Tip 4 **Decide which parts of the passage are most important.**

If you can figure out what's important in the passage, you'll be able to figure out the main idea.

If you summarized as you read, you probably already know what the most important parts of the passage are. On the following lines, list four important parts of "Anansi and His Dinner Guest."

5. _____

_____

_____

6. _____

_____

_____

7. _____

_____

_____

8. _____

_____

_____

Tip 5 **Look for sentences that tell about the main idea.**

9. Look back at the story on pages 8 and 9. Underline the sentence or sentences that tell about the main idea readers should get from the passage.

10. Finish the following discussion by writing the main idea of the Anansi story in your own words.

YOU: "Hey, I read a cool story in class today."

YOUR FRIEND: "Oh, yeah? What was it about?"

YOU: _____

_____

_____

Now that you have written the main idea in your own words, try to find it in the answer choices for Number 11.

11. What is the main idea of the passage?
    A. Turtle has to wash before Anansi will let him eat.
    B. Anansi finishes his supper before Turtle gets any of it.
    C. Turtle asks Anansi to remove his coat before eating dinner.
    D. Anansi tries to outsmart Turtle, but Turtle gets even with him.

Tip 6 Learn to tell the difference between the main idea and a supporting detail.

Main idea (or main topic) questions ask you what the passage is *mostly* about. Beware of answer choices that are only details from the passage. For example, let's look at Number 11 again. Which of the choices are just supporting details?

Turtle has to wash before Anansi will let him eat (A), but this is not the main idea of the passage. It is only a supporting detail. Remember that Anansi's trouble doesn't start until he visits Turtle.

Anansi sends Turtle to the stream a second time and finishes all the food before he returns (B), but these, too, are only supporting details.

Turtle does ask Anansi to remove his coat (C). This causes the spider to rise to the surface and miss dinner. But Anansi's removing his coat and losing out on a meal is not the main idea.

Choices A, B, and C tell important details that support the main idea, but they do not give readers the "big picture": Anansi tries to outsmart Turtle by not sharing his supper, but later, Turtle gets even with Anansi by tricking him out of an underwater feast (D).

Always look out for answer choices that are just supporting details.

Tip 7 Learn to recognize main idea questions.

Main idea questions can be asked in many ways. Here are a few examples:

    "What is this story mostly about?"

    "Which sentence best summarizes this passage?"

"What is the central idea of this passage?"

With practice, you will be able to spot main idea questions easily.

Tip 8 **The theme is a story's general message or lesson.**

The main idea tells about the particular characters or situations in the passage. The **theme**, on the other hand, refers to the more general meaning of the passage. It applies not only to the characters in the story, but also to people everywhere. Most themes have been written about for hundreds, even thousands, of years. They are messages about life, love, heroism, strength, loneliness, and so on; messages that are understood in every language from English to Arabic, from Norwegian to Ashanti.

Sometimes, the theme is called the **moral** of the story, or the lesson that the story is trying to teach. For example, the lesson of "Anansi and His Dinner Guest" is that if you try to outsmart people, they may eventually outsmart you.

12. What is the theme of the story "Anansi and His Dinner Guest"?
    A. Customs are the same everywhere.
    B. Hunger is a worldwide problem.
    C. Trickery usually gets you nowhere.
    D. Washing is important before meals.

What's the Big Idea?
Lesson 1 Summary

When answering main idea or theme questions, remember the following tips:

- Many passages have one clear main idea.
- Sometimes you have to piece together important ideas that lead you to a main idea.
- Summarize the passage as you read.
- Decide which parts of the passage are most important.
- Look for sentences that tell about the main idea.
- Learn to tell the difference between the main idea and a supporting detail.
- Learn to recognize main idea questions.
- The theme is a story's general message or lesson.

Sample Main Idea and Theme Questions

Directions: Use "Anansi and His Dinner Guest" and "The Trickster" on pages 8 and 9 to answer the following questions.

1. What is the topic of the boxed information titled "The Trickster"?
   A. African folktales
   B. folktale tricksters
   C. North American folk heroes
   D. Daffy Duck and Bugs Bunny

2. What is the main idea of the information in the box titled "The Trickster"?
   A. Bugs Bunny is a better trickster than Daffy Duck.
   B. Anansi the spider is a trickster from West African tales.
   C. Trickster characters appear in folktales from many lands.
   D. Tricksters appear in Japanese and South American folktales.

3. Which lesson can be learned from "Anansi and His Dinner Guest"?
   A. Two heads are better than one.
   B. Birds of a feather flock together.
   C. Where there's smoke, there's fire.
   D. Unkind actions may not be forgotten.

4. Which title best tells the main idea of this passage?
   A. "Turtle Gets Even"
   B. "Wash Before Eating"
   C. "Spiders and Turtles"
   D. "Anansi and His Friends"

Additional Practice Questions

5. Look at the graphic organizer and answer the question that follows.

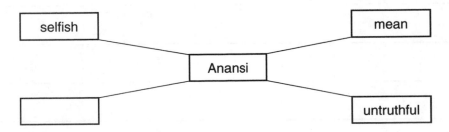

Which word best fits in the empty box?
A. kind   C. happy
B. wise   D. foolish

6. Why does Anansi invite Turtle to share his supper?

    A. He wants to be friendly.

    B. He knows that Turtle is hungry.

    C. He wants to follow his country's custom.

    D. He has more than enough food to share.

7. When summarizing this passage, which of these details would be most important?

    A. There is a stream at the bottom of the hill.

    B. Turtle carefully walks back to Anansi's on the grass.

    C. After being tricked by Anansi, Turtle invites the spider to dinner.

    D. Turtle's dinner includes a platter containing many kinds of fish.

8. Most of the settings and events in this story involve

    A. food.   C. trails.

    B. trees.   D. rocks.

9. The passage says that "Turtle's head <u>emerged</u> from the water." What does the word *emerged* mean?

    A. took in   C. sped up

    B. came out   D. sat down

10. Which character (Anansi or Turtle) seems the kinder and more likeable? Support your answer with details from the passage.

_____

_____

_____

_____

_____

_____

_____

Lesson 2

Details, Details, Details

Try to imagine a story or article without any details.

nce upon a time, in a land far away, some kids had an adventure. They ran into big trouble. They lived through it.

The End

SOMEPLACE, U.S.A.—Today an important event happened. It will cause other things to happen. It is likely to affect someone, somewhere, sometime.

An eyewitness, Mr. Somebody-or-other, told reporters, "Something happened today. I saw it. It was really something."

As you can see, without details, stories are pretty dull!

Details make a story seem real. They make a scary story seem really scary or a funny story really funny. When a story has lots of details, you can almost "see" the story happening right in front of you as you read.

Details in nonfiction books and articles help you understand the topic and the main ideas. The more details the author gives you, the more you will learn about the topic, and the better you will understand the main idea.

Answering Detail Questions

Answering detail questions is like searching for hidden pirate's treasure, except that the treasure isn't really hidden. It's sitting out in the open, just waiting for a treasure hunter (you) to come along and pick it up. Read on to learn clues for finding answers to detail questions.

Treasure Here

Tip 1   **Read the entire passage, making a mental map.**

Read the passage from beginning to end. You don't have to memorize every detail. (Remember, the passage will be in front of you as you answer the questions.)

The important thing is to get a general idea about where things are located in the passage. That way, you will know where to look to find answers to the questions.

Think of this as making a map of the passage—a mental map. You are scouting out the territory, studying the "lay of the land." After you have read the entire passage, you will be ready to start your search for the answer to any detail question thrown your way.

Read the following passage and make a mental map as you go.

Truth and Fiction:
The Story of Two Unsinkable Ships
by Larry Lorrie

She was the largest craft afloat and the greatest of the works of men. In her construction and maintenance were involved every science, profession, and trade. On her bridge were officers . . . who had passed rigid examinations in all studies that pertained to winds, tides, currents, and geography of the sea . . .

From the bridge, engine-room, and a dozen places on her deck, the ninety-two doors of nineteen water-tight compartments could be closed in half a minute by turning a lever . . .

Unsinkable—indestructible, she carried as few [life]boats as the law allowed.

—*Morgan Robertson, "Futility," 1898*

1   Sounds like the *Titanic*, you say? Nope. This imaginary ship, the *Titan*, was sailing the North Atlantic 14 years before the *Titanic* made its only voyage.

2   Here is a very strange trip into the imagination of Morgan Robertson. He lived a long time ago, from 1861 to 1915, and was mostly a writer of sea stories. One of his stories lives on, not because of the quality of its

writing, but because it unknowingly told the strange future of a nearly identical ship built more than 10 years after Robertson's story was published.

3   Have you seen the film *Titanic*? The movie is based on the story of a real luxury ocean liner that was thought to be unsinkable because of its series of watertight compartments. On its very first voyage, traveling through North Atlantic waters, the *Titanic* struck an iceberg and sank. More than 1,500 people went down with the ship on that cold April morning.

4   In 1898, 14 years before the sinking of the *Titanic*, Morgan Robertson wrote and published a short story called "Futility." It was about a large, luxurious ocean liner that he called the *Titan*. The *Titan* was about the same length as the *Titanic* would be, could hold as many passengers as the *Titanic* would hold, and could travel at the same speed as the *Titanic*. It, too, was considered unsinkable because of its watertight compartments— Robertson's fictional *Titan* had 19 compartments, while the real *Titanic* had 15. Both the real ocean liner and its fictional partner had enough lifeboats for only a fraction of the passengers.

The Fictional Ship *Titan* (1898) and the Real Ship *Titanic* (1912)

Category	Robertson's *Titan*	Actual *Titanic*
Country of Origin	Great Britain	Great Britain
Length	800 feet	882.5 feet
Displacement	45,000 tons	66,000 tons
Top speed	25 knots	24–25 knots
Passenger capacity	3,000	3,000
Passengers aboard	3,000	over 2,200
Lifeboats aboard	24	20
Propellers	3	3
Month of sinking	April	April
Time of impact	Around midnight	11:40 P.M.
Cause of sinking	Iceberg	Iceberg
Area of damage	Starboard (right) forward	Starboard (right) forward

5   Robertson's *Titan* was traveling from New York to Southampton, England; the real *Titanic* was going from Southampton, England, to New York. Both ships were traveling the dangerous, icy North Atlantic waters during the month of April. Both ships struck icebergs along the starboard (right) side. And both accidents happened around midnight.

6   After the *Titanic* sank in the early morning hours of April 15, 1912, Robertson's 14-year-old story was republished. The recent success of the movie has renewed interest in Robertson's tale, because the story of his fictional ship *Titan* so closely resembles the story of the real ship *Titanic*.

7   Robertson was the author of many sea stories, though "Futility" is the only one that lives on. His background gave him a special knowledge of the sea. He was born in Oswego, New York, in 1861, the son of a ship captain who worked on the Great Lakes. Robertson later spent nine years in the Merchant Marine, traveling the world on ships. After leaving the Merchant Marine, he worked for a while as the owner of a small jewelry business. After failure in that line of work, he turned to writing. In the next 15 years, he wrote more than 200 stories and published 14 books.

8   Ocean adventure stories were popular with readers back in 1898. Sea travel was common in an era when airplanes had yet to be invented, and there was a certain romance about life at sea. Though "Futility" was seen as adventure writing in its day, Robertson's ability to write about things that would actually happen in the future gives the book an eerie sense of prediction, too. ❖

Tip 2 **Determine which details are important.**

Important details are those that support the main idea of the passage.

1.   Which sentence best summarizes this passage?

A.   The fictional ship *Titan* is very similar to the real ship *Titanic* in both its design and fate.

B.   The author of "Futility" traveled the world on ships during his years in the Merchant Marines.

C.   The movie *Titanic* is based on the true story of a luxury ocean liner that sank after striking an iceberg.

D.   The fictional ship *Titan* had too few lifeboats for the number of passengers it had onboard.

Once you've identified the main idea of the passage, think about which details are most important in supporting the main idea.

2. Which of the following details best supports the idea that the fictional ship *Titan* and the real ship *Titanic* were strikingly similar?

   A. Morgan Robertson was a writer of popular sea stories.

   B. Airplanes had not yet been invented when Robertson's *Titan* story was written.

   C. The author of "Futility" was the son of a ship captain who worked on the Great Lakes.

   D. The *Titan* and the *Titanic* were both built with watertight compartments to keep them from sinking.

3. Return to the passage and find two more details that support the main idea. Write these details on the following lines.

   _____

   _____

   _____

   _____

Tip 3 **Identify key words (clue words) in the question.**

What if you went on a treasure hunt without knowing what you were looking for? It would be difficult to find something if you didn't know what you were looking for.

When answering detail questions, you should know exactly what you are searching for. So, read the question very carefully and look for key words.

Read the following question. Circle the words or groups of words in the sentence that would help you most in finding the answer.

4. How many years before the *Titanic* sailed was Robertson's story "Futility" published?

Tip 4 **Skim the passage for key (important) words from the question.**

Skimming means running your eyes quickly over the page while you are looking for something. You might skim the phone book for the number of your favorite pizza restaurant. You might skim a dictionary for the definition of *mugwump*. When telling a friend about a book you have just read, you might skim through it looking for "a good part" to read aloud.

5. Look at the key words you circled in Number 4. Then go back to the passage and skim for those key words. Whenever you come to one of the key words in the passage, circle it. Then reread each sentence containing the key word or words.

Read the question again. It is reprinted below, this time with answer choices. Circle the correct answer.

6. How many years before the *Titanic* sailed was Robertson's story "Futility" published?
   A. 3 years
   B. 14 years
   C. 19 years
   D. 24 years

Now let's try a few other kinds of detail questions.

7. What made people believe that both the *Titan* and the *Titanic* were unsinkable?
   A. the size of the ships
   B. the ships' expert crews
   C. the number of lifeboats on the ships
   D. the ships' watertight compartments

8. How many lifeboats were aboard the real *Titanic*?
   A. 15
   B. 19
   C. 20
   D. 36

9. What part of Robertson's background gave him special knowledge of the sea?
   A. his experience as a writer
   B. his experience as a jeweler
   C. his experience as a small-business owner
   D. his experience as a sailor in the Merchant Marine

10. What detail from the passage supports the idea that sea stories were popular in 1898?

    A. Ocean travel was common in the era before airplanes.

    B. Most ships of the day were considered to be unsinkable.

    C. Most people made their living by working on ocean liners.

    D. Ships had only recently been invented and were exciting to travelers.

Tip 5 **Answer order-of-events (sequence) questions by skimming the passage for key words from the answer choices. Then relate each event to the others listed.**

"Which came first, the chicken or the egg?"

Detail questions won't be this confusing. But they might ask you about the order of events in a passage—which event happened *first*, *next*, or *last*.

Don't forget, however, that the order of events in a passage can be arranged in different ways:

- **Chronological order** (arranging events in order from earliest to latest based on time) is used quite often to tell the story in fiction and nonfiction narratives.

- **Logical order** usually means the author uses **flashbacks** to previous action, or **foreshadowing** to refer to events that will happen later in the story. This technique is often used in fiction. When logical order is used, the story does not follow a strictly chronological order. The action is arranged for the purpose of making the story more interesting, more exciting, or more understandable to the reader.

- **Sequential order** (arranging the text in a series of steps or actions) is an approach often taken in writing instructions, directions, and other types of nonfiction.

The answer choices are the place to go for clues about order-of-event questions. Find out where each event in the answer choices appears in the passage. To do this, first look for key words in the *choices*. Then skim the passage for these key words. Think about how the event in each choice relates to the other events listed.

11. Which of the following events happened first?

    A. The *Titanic* hit an iceberg and sank in North Atlantic waters.

    B. Morgan Robertson wrote "Futility," a story about a ship that sinks.

    C. The *Titanic* traveled from Southampton, England, to New York.

    D. The story of the *Titanic* was made into a movie that became very successful.

————— Details, Details, Details —————
Lesson 2 Summary

When answering detail questions, remember the following tips:

- Read the entire passage, making a mental map.

- Determine which details are important.

- Identify key words (clue words) in the question.

- Skim the passage for key (important) words from the question.

- Answer order-of-events (sequence) questions by skimming the passage for key words from the answer choices. Then relate each event to the others listed.

Practice Passage

Directions: Read the passage, then answer the questions that follow.

from

Young Ladies Don't Slay Dragons
by Joyce Hovelsrud

A dragon with exceedingly evil intentions was plaguing[1] the Palace of Hexagon. Night and day he <u>lurked about</u> the courtyard walls, belching fire and smoke and roaring in a most terrible fashion. Things looked bad for the royal household.

"Mercy," said the queen.

"Dear me," said the king. "One of these days he'll get a royal blaze going, and when he does—poof! That'll be it."

"Well, what are you going to do about it?" asked the queen sharply. "I mean, you can't just sit there counting out your money and ignoring the problem."

"I have asked every brave man in the kingdom to slay the dragon," said the king. "They all said they had more important things to do."

---

[1] **plaguing:** causing worry or trouble

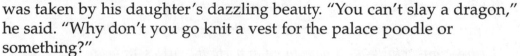

"Nonsense," said the queen with a breathy sigh. "What could be more important than saving the palace from a monstrous dragon? Perhaps you should offer a reward."

"I *have* offered a reward," said the king. "No one seems interested."

"Well then, offer something of value to go with it," said the queen. And with that, she slammed the honey jar on the table and stomped out of the room.

"I'll slay the dragon," said the Princess Penelope, jumping from behind an antique suit of armor. There, she had just happened to be listening to the conversation while oiling a rusty joint.

The king blinked his eyes twice—once with shock because he was taken by surprise, and once with pride because he was taken by his daughter's dazzling beauty. "You can't slay a dragon," he said. "Why don't you go knit a vest for the palace poodle or something?"

The princess flexed the arm of the ancient armor. "See? No more clink." She smiled.

"No more clink," said the king vacantly.

"And I just fixed the drawbridge, too," said the princess. "You won't have to worry about the clank anymore."

"Clink, clank, clunk," said the king. "I have more important worries anyway."

"I know," said Penelope. "The dragon. I *said* I'd slay him for you."

"Nonsense," said the king. "Young ladies don't slay dragons."

"They don't oil armor or fix drawbridges, either," said the princess matter-of-factly.

The king scratched his head and thought about that for a while. Princess Penelope was always giving him something to think about. ❖

Sample Detail Questions

1. Which of the following details about the dragon makes him appear threatening to the king?

   A. He roars, and he belches fire and smoke.

   B. He snores loudly and keeps the palace awake.

   C. He sometimes starts "royal blazes" in the palace.

   D. He has crossed the drawbridge and entered the palace.

2. The details of this story best support which of the following as a good title?
   A. "Clink, Clank, Clunk"
   B. "A Vest for the Poodle"
   C. "Fixing the Drawbridge"
   D. "Penelope Proves Her Point"

3. The main reason the author mentions the detail about Princess Penelope oiling the armor is to show that she
   A. cares for her father.
   B. can do more than "knit."
   C. likes to have well-kept armor.
   D. likes to hide behind the armor.

4. Which sentence from the story best shows that the king doesn't think Penelope can slay the dragon?
   A. *"One of these days he'll get a royal blaze going . . ."*
   B. *"I have offered a reward . . . No one seems interested."*
   C. *"Why don't you go knit a vest for the palace poodle or something?"*
   D. *"Clink, clank, clunk . . . I have more important worries anyway."*

5. What do readers know about the king based on the details in this passage?

   _____

   _____

   _____

   _____

   _____

Additional Practice Questions

6. Which word best describes Penelope?
   A. foolish
   B. confident
   C. confused
   D. frightened

7. In paragraph 1, what is the meaning of the phrase *lurked about*?
   A. burned up
   B. hung around
   C. banged upon
   D. walked away from

8. What is the the king's main problem?
   A. Penelope wants to fight the dragon.
   B. There are no brave men in the kingdom.
   C. A fire-breathing dragon is threatening the castle.
   D. The queen is upset with him and his lack of action.

9. What will most likely happen to solve the king's problem?
   A. The queen will hire a knight to slay the dragon.
   B. Princess Penelope will go out to fight the dragon.
   C. The king will fight the dragon in his antique armor.
   D. The dragon will get tired and go away from the castle.

10. What is the setting for the story?
    A. inside a castle at an unknown time
    B. inside a castle courtyard in the present
    C. on a castle drawbridge about 100 years ago
    D. outside the walls of a castle in a future time

11. Why does the queen slam the honey jar on the table and stomp out of the room?
    A. She is afraid of the fire-breathing dragon.
    B. She is concerned about her daughter's safety.
    C. She is angry because of fire damage done to the castle.
    D. She is unhappy with her husband's lack of action to fix the problem.

12. This story is told from whose point of view?
    A. Penelope
    B. the queen
    C. the king
    D. a narrator who is not part of the story

Lesson 3

Be a Word Detective

The *conifers* started to move—really move. They leaned over the path, *grappling* for the *hobbit* with their *scraggly* limbs as he *galumphed* through the *weald*.

You may be thinking, *Huh? What does this mean?* Take a look at this version:

The *evergreen trees* started to move—really move. They leaned over the path, *grasping* for the *small, human-like creature* with their *ragged* limbs as he *walked clumsily* through the *forest*.

Well, why didn't you say so?

But we did! English is a wonderful language, chock-full of all sorts of unusual words (like *chock-full*). You are sure to run into a few unfamiliar words once in a while.

Of course, you probably won't see words that are as difficult as *galumphed* or *weald* on a reading test. But you might see a few words that are unfamiliar to you. Some of the questions might even ask you the meaning of an unfamiliar word.

So, how are you supposed to learn the meanings of all the words that might be on a test? Here's a shocker: *You don't have to*. A few unfamiliar words won't make a whole passage seem like it's written in Greek. But what about those pesky vocabulary questions?

For vocabulary questions, you need a plan. And, of course, plans are our specialty. Read on to learn some tips for answering vocabulary questions, *even when you don't know the meanings of the words.*

Tip 1 **Find the vocabulary word in the passage.**

Whenever you come to a vocabulary question, the first thing you should do is go back and find the word in the passage. Then read the sentence in which the word appears. You may even want to read a few sentences before and after the unfamiliar word. Then use one of the following tips to help you figure out the word's meaning.

Tip 2 **Look for other words that mean the same thing (synonyms).**

Sometimes the passage will contain other words that have meanings similar to the word you are trying to figure out. You may recall that such words are called **synonyms**.

Read the following passage and answer Numbers 1 and 2.

> Brooke had planned the perfect escape: a tightrope stretched from her bedroom window to the huge, gnarly oak tree outside. Now she would put her plan into action. She climbed out of the window and <u>gingerly</u> stepped onto the rope—first one foot, then the other— carefully adjusting her balance. The tree was only a few feet away. If she went very slowly, watching each and every step, she just might make it.

1. Underline any words or phrases in the passage that are similar in meaning to the word *gingerly*.

2. What is the meaning of the word *gingerly*?
   A. boldly
   B. quietly
   C. secretly
   D. carefully

Tip 3 **Look for words that have the opposite meaning (antonyms).**

Sometimes the passage will give you clues to the opposite meaning of a word. A word that is opposite in meaning to another word is called an **antonym**. If you can figure out an unknown word's opposite meaning, you can usually figure out its meaning. Read the following sentence and answer Numbers 3 and 4.

> Although Brody is usually quite charming and polite, he saw his sister's wedding as the perfect opportunity for <u>obnoxious</u> behavior.

3. Underline any words in the sentence that might have the opposite meaning of the word *obnoxious*.

4. What is the meaning of the word *obnoxious*?
   A. sad
   B. horrible
   C. joyful
   D. friendly

Tip 4 Look for the author's use of definition or restatement to figure out an unknown word.

Authors often define or restate ideas in the text to make the information clear to the reader. Think about how the ideas in the following paragraph help define the underlined word.

> They called themselves "**emigrants**" because, as they started their journey, they were actually leaving America. During the early 1840s, the United States ended at the banks of the Missouri River. The region that later would be Kansas and Nebraska had been set aside by the United States government as Indian territory. California was still a northern province of Mexico. The vast wilderness of the Oregon country was claimed jointly by the United States and Great Britain. Gradually these western territories would become part of the United States. But when the first **emigrants** set out, they were entering a foreign land.

—from *Children of the Wild West* by Russell Freedman

5. What is the meaning of the word *emigrant* as it is used in this paragraph?
   A. people who left their own country to live elsewhere
   B. people who traveled no farther than the Missouri River
   C. people who lived only on land that was part of Great Britain
   D. people who lived only on land that was part of the United States

Tip 5 Look for similar examples of the word in the text.

Words in a series (or list) often give you clues to the meaning of an unknown word in that series. Read the following paragraph and answer Numbers 6 and 7.

> As the morning passed, the hikers saw firs, cedars, maples, pines, and one tall <u>chinquapin</u>. They also observed many blue jays, swallows, and robins, one <u>junco</u>, and two bald eagles.

6. What is the meaning of the word *chinquapin* as it is used in this paragraph?

   A. a kind of river

   B. a kind of lake

   C. a kind of tree

   D. a kind of town

7. What is the meaning of the word *junco* as it is used in this paragraph?

   A. a kind of dog

   B. a kind of cat

   C. a kind of bug

   D. a kind of bird

Tip 6 **Look for word clues in sentences or paragraphs that describe cause and effect.**

Often, when a writer explains a cause-and-effect situation, the situation itself will help you figure out an unknown word. Read the following sentence and answer Number 8.

> After the river overflowed its banks two years in a row, state officials decided to build a dam to <u>avert</u> future flooding.

8. What is the meaning of the word *avert* as it is used in this cause-and-effect sentence?

   A. avoid

   B. unlock

   C. increase

   D. improve

Tip 7 **Plug in answer choices to replace the unknown word.**

If none of the previous tips lead you to the answer, try this strategy. Plug the answer choices into the sentence in place of the unknown word. The choice that makes the most sense in the passage is likely to be the correct answer.

Read the following passage.

> Charles sat fidgeting in the waiting room. His dental appointment was set for 10:00 A.M., but his mother had insisted that they get there early, "just in case Dr. Traymer is running ahead of schedule." So for thirty minutes Charles had been sitting there—thinking about the

dental chair, listening to the sound of the drill down the hall. He didn't think he could <u>withstand</u> it much longer.

Now read Number 9, but DON'T answer it yet.

9. What is the meaning of the word *withstand* as it is used in the paragraph?
   A. hope
   B. moan
   C. wiggle
   D. endure

Now plug each of the choices into the original sentence where the unknown word occurs.
   A. He didn't think he could <u>hope</u> it much longer.
   B. He didn't think he could <u>moan</u> it much longer.
   C. He didn't think he could <u>wiggle</u> it much longer.
   D. He didn't think he could <u>endure</u> it much longer.

Think about the details in the passage. Charles is fidgeting. He's listening to the sound of the drill. He seems to be getting more and more worried. Which answer choice makes the most sense in the original sentence? Go back to Number 9 and circle the letter of the correct answer.

Tip 8 **Look out for words with more than one meaning or words that sound the same, but have different meanings and spellings.**

Many words are spelled the same, but have more than one meaning. These words are called **homonyms** or **homographs**. Take *bug*, for example. A bug might be a little creepy-crawly creature with glassy eyes and six fuzzy legs. Or it might be the way your little sister's actions affect you: "Mom! She's startin' to *bug* me!" There are also words that are spelled the same, have different meanings, and are pronounced differently. A *tear* in your eye is pronounced differently than a *tear* in your jeans.

Some words sound the same, but have different meanings and different spellings. These words are called **homophones**. It's easy to mix up words such as *it's* and *its* or *to*, *too*, and *two*.

The key to answering questions about words is to ask yourself: *How is the author using the word in the passage?* Go back to the passage and reread the sentence containing the unfamiliar word.

Read the following passage and answer Numbers 10 and 11.

Isabel continued to wave to her grandparents as the ship pulled out of the <u>bay</u>. She stood by the railing for what must have been a very long time. She had hardly noticed the ship pick up speed or the spray of water that had begun to dampen her long skirt. She kept her eyes on the shrinking spot of land on the horizon. America would be a long way from Spain, a long way from home.

10. What is the meaning of the word *bay* as it is used in the passage?
    A. a type of picture window
    B. a body of water along a coastline
    C. an animal's howl that is long and loud
    D. a place where cargo is kept on a ship

11. How do you know the answer to Number 10?

    _____

    _____

    _____

Read the following passage and answer Numbers 12 and 13.

Jackie lay curled up in the corner of a cardboard box in the back of the alley, shivering. Tiny icicles were beginning to form on the tips of her black fur. It had been hours since she had last heard the lady's voice calling "Jackie-cat! Here, kitty!" Now all she heard was the <u>bay</u> of hound dogs, the howl of other cats, and the pitter-patter of rain on top of the box.

12. What is the meaning of the word *bay* as it is used in the passage?
    A. a type of picture window
    B. a body of water along a coastline
    C. an animal's howl that is long and loud
    D. a place where cargo is kept on a ship

13. How do you know the answer to Number 12?

    _____

    _____

Tip 9 **Pay attention to extra meanings that certain words have.**

Writers are usually quite careful in the words they choose. They want to communicate a specific idea. All words have a specific meaning or dictionary-type definition called **denotation**. Many words also have an extra meaning called **connotation** that is suggested by how the word is used. A word can have a positive or negative connotation.

The words *unusual* and *odd* both have the following denotative meaning: out of the ordinary. The word *odd*, however, often has a negative connotation that is similar to the meaning of *strange* or *weird*.

Read the following passage and answer Number 14.

> It was a <u>cheap</u>-looking knock-off of an expensive name-brand watch. The "diamonds" looked more like plastic balls than precious stones.

14. What meaning does the author want to indicate with the word *cheap* as it is used in the passage?

   A. reduced

   B. inexpensive

   C. reasonable

   D. low quality

Tip 10 **Use vocabulary clues to understand figurative language.**

If you say that you're so hungry you could eat a horse, you don't mean you could actually eat a 1,000-pound animal. You are using **figurative language** to express how you feel. This is an example of an **idiom**, which is a phrase that doesn't mean exactly what it says. The following are just a few of the hundreds of idioms in the English language.

Idiom	**What It Means**
Leon is **on top of the world**.	Leon is very happy.
I'm in **a pretty pickle**.	I have a real problem.
It was **a long row to hoe**.	It was a long, hard task.

When you come across an idiom in your reading, use the tips you've learned in this lesson to help you figure out its meaning. Pay close attention to the words and sentences around the idioms.

Metaphors and **similes** are also used to create meaning that is different from what is actually being said.

Metaphor	**What It Means**
The lunchroom **was a zoo with loose animals**.	The lunchroom was full of out-of-control students.

Simile	**What It Means**
He's **like a bull in a china shop**.	He's clumsy.

You can often use context to help you figure out the meanings of figurative phrases. Read the following sentence, then answer Number 15.

Ted's room was so messy that trying to find his math homework was <u>like trying to find a needle in a haystack</u>.

15. The phrase *like trying to find a needle in a haystack* means that Ted's homework was

    A. easy to find.   C. too late to find.

    B. hard to find.   D. dangerous to find.

Read the following sentences and write the meaning of each bold-faced idiom on the line provided.

16. I'll get it **by hook or by crook**.

_____

17. The doctor says I'm **fit as a fiddle**.

_____

18. Ebony overslept this morning, and now she's **in hot water**.

_____

19. Paul says his 15-year-old computer **isn't worth a hill of beans**.

_____

20. Don't listen to Carlos. He's **talking through his hat**.

_____

Be a Word Detective
Lesson 3 Summary

When answering vocabulary questions, remember the following tips:

- Find the vocabulary word in the passage.

- Look for other words that mean the same thing (synonyms).

- Look for words that have the opposite meaning (antonyms).

- Look for the author's use of definition or restatement to figure out an unknown word.

- Look for similar examples of the word in the text.

- Look for word clues in sentences or paragraphs that describe cause and effect.

- Plug in answer choices to replace the unknown word.

- Look out for words with more than one meaning or words that sound the same, but have different meanings and spellings.

- Pay attention to extra meanings that certain words have.

- Use vocabulary clues to understand figurative language.

Practice Passage

Directions: Read the passage, then answer the questions that follow.

How to Solve a Mystery
by Kathryn Quin

Have you ever thought about becoming a detective? The following passage tells how a detective-in-training might go about solving everyday mysteries around the house.

1   Disguised as everyday <u>occurrences</u>, such things as missing socks and muddy footprints are actually classic "Whodunit?" cases just waiting to be solved.

2   The case at hand: You find your bicycle, this morning happily stored in the garage, now lying recklessly on the front lawn. Angry? Stop! Don't get angry. Get to the bottom of this puzzle.

3 Like the greatest detectives, you must gather all the facts. You must know *who*, *what*, *when*, *where*, and *why*. Look for clues that may help you find witnesses and, eventually, a suspect.

4 Looking around, you discover two clues: a screwdriver near the bicycle and a big, muddy footprint on the driveway. A closer look <u>reveals</u> that your bicycle seat is missing!

5 Next, you need to find and interview witnesses. People are often the key to solving mysteries. Appear friendly and nonthreatening as you interview them. In general, people do not like to be <u>interrogated</u>. Ask well-thought-out, specific questions so that you can get as much information as possible.

6 "Mom, did you see what happened to my bike? It's lying in a heap on the front lawn," you say. "Did my older brother, 'the handyman,' decide to work on it while I was at practice?"

7 "No, I didn't see anything," your mom says with an odd smile. "Your brother has been at a friend's house since early this morning, and I don't know where your dad went."

8 Since your interview did not solve the case, you decide to investigate your strongest piece of evidence: the footprint. The footprint is pointing directly toward the bike, and a logo in the shape of a star is visible in the print. You search your brain for a list of suspects who wear shoes with a star logo on them. Then you comb the area looking for a matching shoe. Aha! Near the car is a pair of large shoes. You flip one over and find a star logo. But . . . they're your . . . dad's! Could the <u>culprit</u> be your father?

9 *But why*? you wonder. *Why would Dad steal my bicycle seat?*

10 Next, you must consider a motive, the reason a person might have for committing a crime. A motive will connect a specific suspect to the case.

11 This raises a problem. The most obvious <u>suspect</u> is your own father. Still, you can't think of any reason your dad would want to spend his Saturday morning wrecking your bike.

12 "Hi," your dad says, appearing out of nowhere.

13 You decide to go for it. "Dad," you ask angrily, "did you take my . . . "

14 "Take your what?" Dad asks, a slight grin on his face.

15 "Huh? What? Oh, nothing," you reply, staring at the super-gel mountain-bike seat he is holding.

16 "So, do you want to give me a hand attaching this new seat? We can adjust your brakes, too," he says.

17 "Uh, sure. Thanks, Dad," you reply in the most <u>grateful</u> tone you can come up with.

18 Case solved! ❖

Sample Vocabulary Questions

1. What does the word *occurrences* mean as it is used in paragraph 1?
   A. stories
   B. crimes
   C. purchases
   D. happenings

2. What does the word *reveals* mean in paragraph 4?
   A. shows
   B. thinks
   C. searches
   D. understands

3. In paragraph 5, what is the meaning of *interrogated*?
   A. punished
   B. recognized
   C. questioned
   D. interrupted

4. What does the word *culprit* mean as it is used in paragraph 8?
   A. investigator
   B. guilty person
   C. main witness
   D. person interviewed

5. Read the following sentence from the passage.

   The most obvious <u>suspect</u> is your own father.

   In which sentence does the word *suspect* mean the same thing as in the sentence above?
   A. Because he was caught telling a lie, his honesty is now *suspect*.
   B. I *suspect* that you will be able to find peaches in the canned foods aisle.
   C. The sheriff finally arrested the *suspect* after searching for him for weeks.
   D. We *suspect* Carrie to be the person who put a water balloon in Bob's locker.

6. Which of the following words is a synonym for *grateful*?
   A. helpful
   B. hopeful
   C. faithful
   D. thankful

Additional Practice Questions

7. What is this passage mostly about?
   A. looking for Dad
   B. a missing bicycle
   C. famous detectives
   D. solving a mystery

8. Where does most of the action in this passage take place?
   A. a friend's house
   B. inside the garage
   C. in or near a bicycle shop
   D. on or near the front lawn

9. The author of this passage wants the reader to be
   A. taught.
   B. warned.
   C. worried.
   D. frightened.

10. What is the main reason detectives should "appear friendly and nonthreatening" when interviewing witnesses?
    A. because witnesses could become close friends
    B. because witnesses will be more likely to cooperate
    C. because most people expect law officials to be kind
    D. because witnesses often lie to unfriendly detectives

11. Use details from the passage to summarize the best way to solve a mystery.

    _____

    _____

    _____

    _____

    _____

    _____

    _____

    _____

    _____

Lesson 4

What's the Word?

Learning new words is easier than you might think. Anytime you see an unfamiliar word while you are reading, try to figure out what it means by using clues from the passage. Look at the word closely to see if you know some part of the word. This lesson will give you tips for understanding word parts and using word resources to help you build a *monster* vocabulary.

Tip 1 **The meaning of a root word can be changed by adding an affix.**

Many words can be divided into separate parts. The most important part of each word is called the **root word**. In each of the following examples, the root word is in **bold type**.

> **play** + full = playful
>
> un + **wise** = unwise
>
> **hug** + able = huggable

Affixes are word parts that can be added to a root word to change its meaning. There are two kinds of affixes: **prefixes**, which are added to the beginning of a root word, and **suffixes**, which are added to the end of a root word. Sometimes, adding an affix hardly changes the meaning of the root word. Other times, adding an affix changes the meaning a great deal.

Adding a Prefix

Here's an example of a root word with a prefix:

> *un*   +   *ready*   =   *unready*
> (prefix)   (root word)   (new word)

By adding *un* to *ready*, the meaning is changed a great deal. Now, instead of meaning *prepared* (ready), the new word means *not prepared* (*not* ready).

Adding a Suffix

This time, let's add a suffix:

ready + *ness* = *readiness*
(root word)   (suffix)   (new word)

By starting with *ready* and adding *ness*, we didn't change the meaning very much. A person who feels *ready* is in a state of *readiness*.

Adding a Prefix and a Suffix

What happens when we add both the prefix *un* and the suffix *ness* to the base word *ready*? Try it and see:

un + *ready* + *ness* = _____

Which of the following phrases means the same as the new word you just made?

Circle your choice.

the state of being ready   the state of being not ready

By studying the common prefixes and suffixes covered in this lesson, you will be able to figure out the meanings of many new words.

Tip 2 **Prefixes are added to the beginnings of root words.**

Remember, when you add letters to the beginning of words, the add-ons are called **prefixes**. Many words in the English language use prefixes. Here are some of the most common prefixes and their meanings.

Prefix	Meaning	Example
bi	two	bicycle
de	undo/remove	deflate/defrost
dis	away/apart/not	disappear/disagree
ex	out	exhale
im	not/into	impossible/import
in	not	inaccurate
mis	wrongly/badly	misspell
multi	many	multimillion
pre	before	prejudge
semi	half/partly	semicircle/semisoft
un	not	undecided

Practice Activity 1: Prefixes

Directions: For Numbers 1 through 6, add a prefix to the given root word to make a new word.

1. Add a prefix to the root word *sweet* to make a word that means *partly sweet*.

   _____

2. Add a prefix to the root word *cook* to make a word that means *cook before*.

   _____

3. Add a prefix to the root word *like* to make a word that means *not like*.

   _____

4. Add a prefix to the root word *count* to make a word that means *count wrongly*.

   _____

5. Add a prefix to the root word *fog* to make a word that means *remove fog*.

   _____

6. Add a prefix to the root word *vitamin* to make a word that means *many vitamins*.

   _____

Tip 3 **Suffixes are added to the ends of root words.**

When you add letters to the end of words, the add-ons are called **suffixes**.

Here are some common suffixes that you should know.

Suffix	Meaning	Example
ance/ence	fact, state	*dependence*
ation/ition	action, state	*determination*
hood	condition, state	*manhood*
ment	action, result, state	*amazement*
ty/ity	quality of being	*curiosity*
ness	condition, state	*greatness*
able/ible	able to, able to be	*lovable*
ish	like	*girlish*
ous, ious	full of, having	*gracious, mountainous*
fy, ify	make, cause	*fortify*
ize	cause to be	*modernize*
en	to make	*sweeten*
ate	cause to become, make	*activate*

Practice Activity 2: Suffixes

Directions: For Numbers 7 through 15, add a suffix to the given root word to make a new word.

7. Add a suffix to the root word *good* to make a word that means *the condition of being good.*

   _____

8. Add a suffix to the root word *employ* to make a word that means *the state of being employed.*

   _____

9. Add a suffix to the root word *mother* to make a word that means *the state of being a mother.*

   _____

10. Add a suffix to the root word *child* to make a word that means *like a child*.

    _____

11. Add a suffix to the root word *erase* to make a word that means *able to be erased*.

    _____

12. Add a suffix to the root word *nerve* to make a word that means *full of nerves*.

    _____

13. Add a suffix to the root word *sick* to make a word that means *the condition of being sick*.

    _____

14. Add a suffix to the root word *wide* to make a word that means *to make wide*.

    _____

15. Add a suffix to the root word *standard* to make a word that means *cause to be standard*.

    _____

Tip 4 **Some suffixes indicate verb tense, singular and plural nouns, and whether a word is an adjective or an adverb.**

This tip probably sounds complicated, but it's not. The following types of word endings are called **inflectional suffixes**, and you read them all the time.

Verb suffixes such as *-ed*, *-ing*, *-en*, and *-s* show verb tense (look*ed*, danc*ing*, ridd*en*, talk*s*).

The noun suffix *-s* shows that a noun is plural (computer*s*, girl*s*, dog*s*).

Adjective suffixes such as *-y*, *-ese*, *-er*, *-est* change nouns and verbs to adjectives or are used to compare adjectives (rock*y*, Vietnam*ese*, long*er*, fast*est*).

Adverb suffixes such as *-ly* or *-ily* show that a word is being used as an adverb (slow*ly*, stead*ily*).

Practice Activity 3: Suffixes

Directions: Circle the word or words in the following sentences that have inflectional suffixes. The first one has been done for you.

16. The (students started running) to their (lockers.)

17. They have forgotten the "no running rule."

18. Larry waits patiently for the bell to ring.

19. Serena is the tallest girl on the team.

20. Alex has a Siamese cat that runs away frequently.

Tip 5 **Use prefixes, suffixes, and roots to take words apart and figure out their meanings.**

Once you've studied common word parts and their meanings, you can figure out the meanings of larger words by breaking them down into parts.

For example, let's take the word *unknowable* apart:

unknowable = un + know + able

Un means "not," and *able* means "able to be," so *unknowable* must mean "not able to be known."

Now you try.

Practice Activity 4: Taking Words Apart

Directions: For Numbers 21 through 23, break up the given word into its root and affix(es). Then give the meaning of the word.

21. enjoyable = _____ + _____

    Meaning: _____

22. fatherhood = _____ + _____

    Meaning: _____

23. discouragement = _____ + _____ + _____

Meaning: _____

Tip 6 **English is made up of words from almost every language.**

English has more words than any other language. This is because English has taken words from many other languages. Many words you see and use every day originally came from other languages. Here are some examples:

- squash, tomato, chocolate, potato, chipmunk, Ohio (Native American languages)

- coyote, rodeo, lasso, banana, patio, cafeteria, buffalo (Spanish)

- prairie, pioneer, gopher, dime, cent, Vermont (French)

- typhoon, judo, karate, karaoke (Japanese)

- tea, wonton, chopstick, soy, chow (Chinese languages)

- boomerang, kangaroo (Australian Aboriginal languages)

- golf, boy, Yankee, waffle, cookie, caboose (Dutch)

- hamburger, noodle, waltz, poodle, kindergarten (German)

- chimpanzee, gumbo, banjo, banana, yam, zebra (African languages)

And when there isn't a word from another language that quite fits, English often comes up with new words by combining old ones. For example, when people needed a word for the cloudy, misty haze that was caused by factories and car exhaust in big cities, the words *smoke* and *fog* were combined to make the word *smog*.

Don't Be Stumped by Abbreviations (abbr)

Writers sometime use short versions of words when they write. You're probably quite familiar with the abbreviations for the days of the week (Mon, Tues, Wed, Thurs, Fri, Sat, Sun), states (OH, CA, NY, IL, MI), and many other common terms such as chap. (chapter), in. (inch), ft. (foot), ex. (example), etc. (et cetera), and govt. (government). There are an endless number of words that can be abbreviated, so you won't be able to memorize them all. You can, however, pay attention to how the abbreviation is used in the sentence or paragraph. The writer will usually leave you plenty of clues. See if you can figure out the abbreviations used in the following sentence:

She <u>recd</u> a speeding ticket for going 75 <u>mph</u> on <u>Hwy</u> 33 on her way to the capitol <u>bldg</u> in <u>OH</u>.

⬛ *Tip 7* **Many English words come from Latin and Greek.**

Most dictionary entries tell the origin of each word, so as you look up a word, check to see where it came from originally. Here's an example of a dictionary definition.

> **ex' port** /ek' spōrt/*verb* [from Latin *exportare*: to carry]
> **1**: to carry away **2**: to carry or send to some other place
> (as another country)

Many of our common words come from Latin and Greek. One reading specialist has estimated that knowing just a few common Latin and Greek roots could help a reader understand thousands of English words. Here are several prefixes and roots that will help you determine the meanings of unknown words.

Latin and Greek Prefixes and Roots

Some Common Latin Prefixes and Roots			
bi (two)	biceps	bifocal	bicycle
cor (heart)	core	courage	encourage
dict (say)	dictate	diction	predict
fin (end)	final	finish	confine
mal (bad)	malady	malice	malformed
port (carry)	export	import	transport
trans (across, over)	transfer	transcribe	transport
uni (one)	unicorn	uniform	unite
Some Common Greek Prefixes and Roots			
auto (self)	autobiography	automobile	automatic
bio (life)	biography	biology	bionic
gram, graph (write)	diagram	telegram	graphic
micro (small)	microbe	microfilm	microscope
phon (sound)	telephone	phonics	symphony
syn, sym (together)	synonym	sympathy	syntax
tele (far, distant)	telegraph	telescope	television

24. Using the table, determine the meaning of the word *transport*.

_____

25. Using the table, determine the meaning of the word *telephone*.

_____

Tip 8 **Use resources within a text, such as glossaries, footnotes, and sidebars, to find the meanings of unknown words.**

Glossary

A **glossary** is an alphabetical listing that defines important words used in a book. Glossaries generally appear at the back of textbooks and other reference books. Here is part of a glossary from a 5th-grade science book.

---

absorb: to soak up, like a sponge (page 18)

adapt: to change in a way that helps a species to survive; it usually takes a long time and many generations for organisms to adapt (pages 47, 51)

amphibian: a cold-blooded vertebrate that lays eggs, has three stages of life, and can live on land or in water (pages 50, 54)

attract: to pull something using a force such as magnetic force (pages 12, 33, 40)

axis: the imaginary line that connects the North and South Poles; the Earth rotates on its axis (pages 41, 79)

bar graph: a picture used to compare like kinds of data (pages 13, 41, 76)

boiling: the process of changing from a liquid state to a gas state by adding heat energy (page 17)

---

26. What best defines the word *attract* as it is used in this science book?

    A. to be charming towards someone

    B. to influence someone in a powerful way

    C. to use force in pulling something toward another object

    D. to connect the North Pole to the South Pole using force

Footnotes

Footnotes are small notes at the bottom of a page. These notes explain, define, or expand on information in the text. A word is marked for a footnote by a small raised number or symbol following the word or sentence (Example: dolmen[1]). A matching number or symbol will guide the reader to an explanation or definition at the bottom of the page. An example is shown at the bottom of this paragraph. You'll have several opportunities to use footnotes in this workbook.

[1] **dolmen:** a prehistoric monument of two or more stones supporting a table-like slab of stone. Found in France and Great Britain, they are thought to mark ancient graves.

What's in a Sidebar?

Authors sometimes use sidebars to highlight additional information that will help the reader better understand the main story or article. (See page 9 for the sidebar called "The Trickster.") Throughout this workbook, you will find sidebars such as the one you are reading. Read the sidebar information carefully—it often defines a word or a concept that will help you better understand the material you're reading.

Tip 9 **Use dictionaries and thesauruses to find word meanings and pronunciations.**

Dictionary

A **dictionary** is a book about words. A dictionary of the American language contains English words that are spoken in the United States, their definitions, and other information.

Some of the information that can be found in dictionaries includes the following:

- correct spellings
- pronunciations
- definitions
- parts of speech (verb, noun, adjective, and so on)
- where the word came from
- an example of the word used in a sentence

Practice Activity 5: Dictionary

Directions: The following dictionary meanings show different ways that the word *leave* is used as a verb to show action. Following each sentence, write the meaning number that best describes the way *leave* is being used.

> **leave** (lēv), *verb*. **1** cause to remain: *The grape juice will leave a stain.* **2** fail to take: *Don't leave your lunchbox at home.* **3** allow: *Leave everything to me.* **4** abandon: *Leave the car in the ditch.* **5** deposit: *Leave the package on the front porch.*

27. That cut will leave a scar. _____

28. Leave your coat in the closet. _____

29. Did you leave your notebook at school? _____

30. He plans to leave one friend for another. _____

31. Leave the thinking to me. _____

Thesaurus

A **thesaurus** gives lists of words with similar meanings. If you wanted to find a word that means the same thing as *aid*, a thesaurus or a dictionary of synonyms would be a good place to look. A thesaurus entry might look like this:

> **aid:** (*noun*) help, assistance, relief, helping hand, support; (*verb*) help, assist, relieve, lend a hand; (*adjective*) helpful, useful; (*adverb*) helpfully, usefully

32. Which word is a synonym for *aid* that can be used as a verb?
    A. useful
    B. relief
    C. relieve
    D. helpfully

What's the Word?
Lesson 4 Summary

When answering questions about word understanding, remember the following tips:

- The meaning of a root word can be changed by adding an affix.
- Prefixes are added to the beginnings of root words.
- Suffixes are added to the ends of root words.
- Some suffixes indicate verb tense, singular and plural nouns, and whether a word is an adjective or an adverb.
- Use prefixes, suffixes, and roots to take words apart and figure out their meanings.
- English is made up of words from almost every language.
- Many English words come from Latin and Greek.
- Use resources within a text, such as glossaries, footnotes, and sidebars, to find the meanings of unknown words.
- Use dictionaries and thesauruses to find word meanings and pronunciations.

Practice Passage

Directions: Read the passage, then answer the questions that follow.

Health Fads
by Linda Houston

1   There is a lot of talk these days about the cost of doctors, hospitals, and health care. Americans spend more money on their health than any other people in the world. We also spend enormous amounts of money on diets, fads, and gimmicks that we think will make us healthier.

2   Health fads in America became very popular about a hundred years ago. At that time, many people lived to be only about 40 years old. Professional medical care was not regulated.[1] Doctors did not have to be as strictly trained as they are today. In addition, most men smoked. Women wore corsets and figure-molding garments that weighed 15 pounds or more. These garments restricted their breathing and often harmed their internal organs. People rarely bathed. Sheets and bed clothes were not changed often. Homes had bugs. The streets were filthy. There was no refrigeration and there were no electric <u>lights</u>. Food was not preserved to keep it fresh and free from germs and disease. All of these factors together caused major health problems.

3   Many of the health fads that came along were actually quite <u>healthful</u>. In the 1830s, Dr. Sylvester Graham said that most people were <u>misinformed</u>. He said major health problems could be solved if people ate less meat and less refined white flour. This was quite a statement since those two elements were eaten at almost every meal. Dr. Graham said fruits, vegetables, and whole-grain wheat were what people needed to be healthy. He made his own flour out of whole-grain wheat. The flour came to be known as "Graham flour." From this flour, Dr. Graham made a thin brown cracker. Although this was the first "graham cracker," it tasted nothing like today's graham crackers. It wasn't until after Dr. Graham's death at age 58 that the crackers were made a bit crisper and sweeter.

4   In 1894, Dr. John Harvey Kellogg, along with his brother, Will Keith Kellogg, invented another health food. The two men were working in Battle Creek, Michigan, trying to come up with a substitute for bread. They created the corn flake. These original flakes tasted like cardboard and were not an immediate hit. It wasn't until Will thought of adding a touch of sweetener to the flakes that they really took off. Advertising genius C. W. Post copied Kellogg's flakes in 1906 and sold hundreds

[1]**regulated:** controlled by rules.

of boxes of his own Post Toasties. Today, there are many varieties of corn flakes. But the original can always be claimed by two brothers who started a craze in the cereal business and helped bring the corn flake to its current success.

5   Not all early health-fad inventors are so <u>memorable</u>. Even most of their products have been forgotten. You've probably never heard of Painless Parker. He was a California dentist whose procedures were anything but painless. He traveled with a small circus, including a brass band, an elephant, and a tattooed lady. While Painless Parker pulled teeth on street corners, the band played to drown out the screams of the patients.

6   Another forgotten fad creator is Bernard MacFadden. At the time, his ideas were considered much too strange to be taken seriously. Today, they are part of our everyday lives. He said people should exercise and wash their entire bodies every day. He believed in walking rather than riding everywhere. He also believed in eating a varied diet. He thought houses should be kept at 70 degrees Fahrenheit in both winter and summer. By following his own beliefs, MacFadden outlived many of his peers. He lived to be 88 years old.

7   Today, many health fads involve dieting to lose weight. Millions of dollars worth of products are sold each year. Cures for all kinds of illnesses are advertised on TV, in newspapers, in magazines, on billboards, on radio . . . everywhere. Many Americans think they should be healthier. Most know that the basics of <u>cleanliness</u>, food <u>preservation</u>, eating right, and getting exercise will help. But the next fad to come along will certainly get everyone's attention. You never know—it just might be the best thing since corn flakes. ❖

Sample Vocabulary Questions

1. As it is discussed in paragraph 2, what best describes the medical care that is not *regulated*?
   A. health care that is a fad
   B. health care that is dangerous
   C. health care that is watched closely
   D. health care that is not strictly controlled by rules

2. In paragraph 2, what does the word *lights* mean?
   A. lamps
   B. sunrises
   C. sets fire to
   D. shines upon

3. In paragraph 3, it says that "many of the health fads that came along were actually quite <u>healthful</u>." What is the meaning of *healthful*?
   A. not healthy
   B. full of health
   C. having poor health
   D. without any health

4. In paragraph 3, the word *misinformed* means
   A. not informed.
   B. fully informed.
   C. partly informed.
   D. wrongly informed.

5. What does the word *memorable* mean in paragraph 5?
   A. able to be remembered
   B. having a good memory
   C. without any memory
   D. hoping to be remembered

6. What is the root word of *cleanliness* in paragraph 7?
   A. an
   B. lean
   C. clean
   D. lines

7. In paragraph 7, the word *preservation* means
   A. unable to serve.
   B. not able to make safe.
   C. the action of preserving.
   D. the action of keeping something cold.

Additional Practice Questions

8. Which of the following best summarizes this passage?

   A. Dr. Sylvester Graham advised people to eat less meat and more fruit, grain, and vegetables. Although his work set some people on the road to an improved diet, he is mostly remembered for inventing graham crackers.

   B. Health fads have long been a part of our society. For nearly two hundred years, Americans have followed the advice of doctors, scientists, and advertisers to become part of a cleaner, healthier society.

   C. There are many benefits in following a health fad. Such fads have resulted in cleaner streets, healthy diets of corn flakes and graham crackers, and dentists who travel with small circuses.

   D. The costs of health care have always been high. Such costs will continue to rise as long as radio, television, magazine, and billboard advertisers are allowed to sell cures for more and more illnesses.

9. The health fads that came along during the 1800s were

   A. always harmful.

   B. sometimes helpful.

   C. laughed at and ignored.

   D. designed around corn flakes.

10. Complete the diagram by writing four examples of conditions that contributed to poor health a hundred years ago.

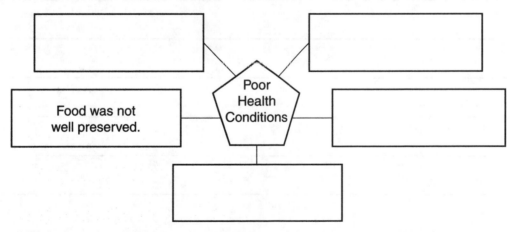

11. What is the author's purpose in paragraph 2?

   A. to persuade the reader that health fads are bad

   B. to entertain the reader with funny stories about health fads

   C. to make the reader angry about how doctors were trained

   D. to inform the reader about what life was like a hundred years ago

12. Which of the following tells how "Graham flour" is different from white flour?

    A. Graham flour is white flour mixed with oats.

    B. Graham flour is made from graham crackers.

    C. Graham flour is made from whole-grain wheat.

    D. There is no difference between the two flours.

13. The author compares the taste of the original corn flakes to which of the following?

    A. bread

    B. cardboard

    C. graham crackers

    D. whole-grain wheat

14. Which of the following statements is an opinion?

    A. There was no refrigeration and there were no electric lights.

    B. The flour came to be known as "Graham flour."

    C. Millions of dollars worth of products are sold each year.

    D. But the next fad to come along will certainly get everyone's attention.

15. Do you agree with the author that some health fads might actually be healthful? Use ideas from the passage to support your answer.

    _____

    _____

    _____

    _____

    _____

    _____

    _____

    _____

    _____

Reading with Understanding

Now we get to dive into all kinds of reading. In this unit, you will first learn some reading strategies that can help you become a better, more-organized reader, even if you're a good reader already. Then you'll find out how writers of fiction develop their interesting stories and see how nonfiction writers present their information. You'll also take a look at poetry (which really *can* be fun), figurative language, and drama.

After you finish this unit, you'll have a better understanding of any kind of reading that comes your way.

In This Unit

◆ *Reading Strategies*
◆ *Made-Up Stories*
◆ *Words That Sing*
◆ *Real People, Events, and Information*

Lesson 5

Reading Strategies

Think about how scary it was the first time you skated. Then, remember how much confidence you gained when you could balance properly without falling. Now, think about how you skate today. Not only is your fear gone, but you're confident and know what to expect. Skating is probably very enjoyable now that you know how to do it.

Reading can be enjoyable, too, especially if you're confident that you know why you're reading, what you're reading, and how to monitor (watch) yourself as you read. You'll learn about all of these skills in this lesson.

Tip 1 **Be aware of your purpose for reading.**

We read for many different purposes. We study textbooks to learn, sometimes memorizing information they contain. We read novels and short stories for pleasure, usually not approaching them with the same amount of concentration. Whether reading to find out or to learn, to understand, to interpret, to enjoy, or to solve problems, we should be prepared to adjust our concentration. This will ensure our full appreciation of the author's work.

1. Which of the following items would probably be read mainly for pleasure?
   A. a road atlas
   B. a short story
   C. a science textbook
   D. a daily newspaper

2. Which of the following could be read to help you make something?
   A. a cookbook
   B. a comic book
   C. a telephone book
   D. a newspaper editorial

Tip 2 Look over the passage or book and predict what it will be about.

When you know what to expect in a passage, reading can be easier and more enjoyable, too. Before you begin reading, scan the passage. See if you can **predict** (make an educated guess about) what it will be about. Here are some text features to look for when you preview a passage or book:

Special type

Many books, encyclopedia entries, and articles of all sorts use **different styles of type** to help organize the material they are presenting. Here are a few of those special styles.

Common styles of type

roman (regular) type

italic type

bold-faced type

underlined type

CAPITAL LETTERS

a combination of any *or* **ALL OF** <u>*these styles*</u>

Title and author

Most written works have a name. That name is called a **title**. The title is usually printed in larger type than any other text in the story, article, book, or poem. It usually appears with the **author's name**.

Headings and subheadings

Headings and **subheadings** act as subtitles throughout the written work. They break the passage or chapter into small parts and let the reader know what is coming next. For example, a magazine article about video games might have sections of the article under such headings as:

Sports Games   **Maze Games**   **Other Games**

Headings allow readers to skim the article and easily find the kind of information that is most important to them.

Visual information, captions, and footnotes

Look at any pictures, illustrations, charts, graphs, or tables that go with the passage. **Captions** are found under or beside illustrations. They are sentences or short paragraphs that explain the contents of a photograph, drawing, graph, or chart.

Check to see if there are footnotes at the bottom of the page explaining words or concepts in the passage.

3. Preview the passage that follows on pages 59 and 60. (Later in the lesson, you will have a chance to read it carefully.) What do you think it will be about?

_____

_____

_____

4. How does the author break the story into parts?

_____

_____

_____

5. What is the most likely purpose for reading this passage?
   A. to be entertained by an interesting story
   B. to find out information about treating croup
   C. to solve a medical problem of your own
   D. to learn about family doctors during the 1800s

6. How does the author let the reader know what *croup* is?
   A. with a picture
   B. with a footnote
   C. with a subhead
   D. with a separate paragraph

Anne to the Rescue

adapted from Lucy Maud Montgomery's *Anne of Green Gables*

The Request

1   Just as Anne came up from the cellar with a plateful of apples for Uncle Matthew, she heard the sound of footsteps on the icy boardwalk outside the kitchen door. In rushed Anne's friend and neighbor Diana Barry, white-faced and out of breath.

2   "What on earth is the matter, Diana?" cried Anne.

3   "Oh, Anne, do come quick. Minnie May is awful sick—she's got croup[1] and can't breathe right. The baby-sitter says it's really bad, and Mother and Father are away in town. Oh, Anne, I'm so scared!"

4   Without a word, Uncle Matthew grabbed his coat and headed to the barn. Anne knew he was planning to saddle the mare and ride to Carmody for the doctor.

5   "Don't cry, Di," said Anne cheerily. "I know exactly what to do for croup. Don't forget that I helped Mrs. Hammond raise her three pairs of twins—and they had the croup regularly. Here, let me take this bottle of ipecac.[2] You may not have any at your house."

6   The two little girls hurried across the snow-crusted fields to Diana's house. The night was clear and frosty, and big stars were shining.

The Cure

7   When they arrived, they saw that 3-year-old Minnie May was really very sick. She lay on a sofa in the kitchen, feverish and restless. Mary Joe, the baby-sitter, was helpless—unable to think and unable to act even if she could have thought properly.

8   Anne went to work with speed and skill.

9   "She's bad, but I've seen worse. First we need hot water and lots of soft flannel cloths. Diana, you and Mary Joe see to that. I'm gonna dose Minnie May with this ipecac."

10   The ipecac went down many times during that long night. As Anne worked with patience over the suffering child, the other girls kept up a

[1] **croup:** a sickness that causes difficult breathing and a severe cough
[2] **ipecac:** a syrupy medicine once used to cure croup

roaring fire and heated enough water for a hospital full of sick babies.

11 It was three o'clock in the morning when Matthew arrived with the doctor. But the emergency was over. Minnie May was sleeping soundly.

An Astonished Doctor

12 "I was awfully near giving up," Anne explained to the doctor. "I thought she was going to choke to death. I gave her every ounce of ipecac in that bottle and when the last dose went down I said to myself, 'This is the last hope.' But, in about three minutes, she coughed until her lungs were clear and then she began to get better. You can just imagine my relief, doctor. You know there are some things that cannot be expressed in words."

13 "Yes, I know," nodded the doctor. He looked at Anne as if he were thinking some things about *her* that couldn't be expressed, either.

14 Leading the mare, Anne and Matthew walked home in the wonderful, white-frosted winter morning. They crossed the long white fields, walked under a glittering fairy arch of frosty maples, and returned to the cozy warmth of Green Gables. ❖

Tip 3 **Determine what genre (type of writing) you are reading.**

A **genre** is a style or kind of literature. Your purpose for reading in these various genres will differ. Sometimes you will read to be entertained. You may read nonfiction to learn about a certain subject. And sometimes you will read simply because you like the author's style or because someone recommends a book to you. Writings within each genre tend to follow the same general organization and have the same qualities. There are, however, different types of writings within each genre.

- **Fiction** tells a made-up story using characters and conversations. One common form of fiction is the chapter book. An example is *Charlotte's Web*, which includes a list of the chapter titles at the front of the book. Some kinds of fiction include the following:

    Realistic fiction (stories that could happen to anyone)

    Fantasy (stories that could never really happen, featuring strange characters and settings)

    Science fiction (stories set in the future or telling a story about humans in a struggle with science and machines)

    Folklore (stories passed down from one generation to another, including **tall tales**, such as "Paul Bunyan and His Blue Ox"; **fairy tales**, such as "Cinderella"; **folktales**, such as "The Ugly Duckling"; **fables**, such as "The Tortoise and the Hare"; and **myths**, such as stories about Hercules)

- **Historical fiction** tells about real people and/or real events but uses some characters, scenes, and conversations that the writer makes up. Books like *Number the Stars* and *Johnny Tremain* are examples of historical fiction.

- **Nonfiction** gives true information about real people, places, things, ideas, and events. Types of nonfiction include the following:

  Biography (a story about someone's life)

  Autobiography (the story of the author's life)

  Fact-based information (such as textbooks, news articles, and instructions)

- **Narratives** are stories told from one person's point of view. They can be either fiction or nonfiction and tend to be told in the order that events happen.

Pass It Along

When you read a book, a poem, or an article that you really like, recommend it to others. Think about who might enjoy it as much as you.

- **Drama** is literature written to be spoken and performed on stage. Works of drama, often called *plays*, tell actors what words to say and how to move about the stage. Some dramas are based on true events; some are about people and events made up by the author. Drama can be written in prose (normal writing) or in poetry. School plays, television sitcoms, and Shakespearean plays are all examples of drama.

- **Poetry** comes in many styles. Some poems tell a story; others simply describe an image or an emotion. Some poems rhyme; some don't. Poems try to express ideas and feelings in unusual ways. Poetry is usually written in groups of lines called *stanzas*.

- **Electronic texts** can be found on numerous Internet websites. Such sites contain literary works in all the genres that have been listed here.

7. Which of the following genres best describes "Anne to the Rescue"?
   A. fiction
   B. poetry
   C. nonfiction
   D. instruction

Tip 4 **Ask yourself questions as you read and check your understanding.**

Don't wait until you have finished reading a passage to try to figure out what it is saying. Ask yourself questions about the passage as you read along: Do I understand this part? Does this really make sense? Why did this happen? Where is this going? What is the main idea of this passage?

8. Carefully read "Anne to the Rescue" on pages 59 and 60. Then write one or two questions about events in the passage that you don't understand or you would like to know more about.

_____

_____

_____

Tip 5 **From time to time, stop to summarize what you have read.**

As you read, stop every now and then. Think back over what you have read. Summarize it in your own words. List the important points in your mind or write them down. This is very helpful when you are reading something complicated. It is always easier to understand something one step at a time than it is to try to understand the "big picture" all at once.

9. Which of the following best summarizes paragraphs 1 through 6?

A. Matthew grabs his coat and heads for the barn. Anne knows that he plans to saddle his horse and ride into town for a doctor.

B. Diana's parents are away in town. She and a baby-sitter have been left to take care of a sick child.

C. Anne comes up from the cellar with a plateful of apples. She hears someone coming. Then her friend Diana rushes in out of breath.

D. Diana rushes to her friend's house and begs Anne to help with a sick baby. Anne grabs a bottle of medicine, and the two girls hurry back to Diana's house.

10. Summarize the part of the story called "The Cure."

_____

_____

_____

_____

_____

To help you interpret your everyday reading, you might do one or more of the following:

- Reread parts that you're having difficulty understanding.
- Keep a journal that summarizes what you have read.
- Discuss what you have read with a friend.
- Watch a television program or a movie about the same subject.
- Visit a library and check out additional books on the subject.
- Use a search engine to find additional information about the subject on the Internet.

Tip 6 **Use graphic organizers to help you understand information.**

Sometimes it is helpful to use a graphic (visual) organizer to sort out and connect important ideas. You can create your own graphic organizers with boxes, circles, ovals, and arrows. Fill in the following diagram and the one on page 64 with information from "Anne to the Rescue."

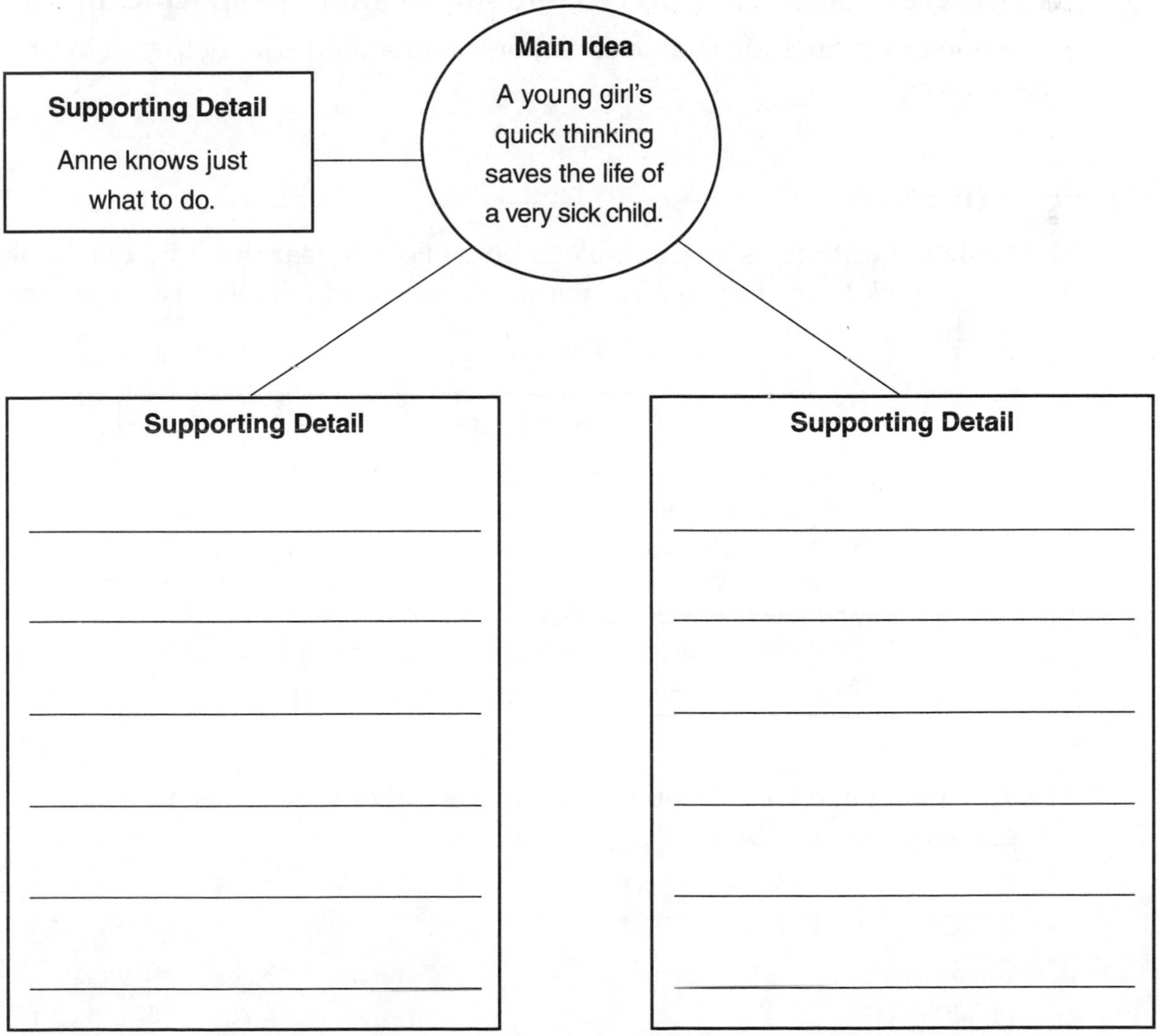

Supporting Detail

Anne knows just what to do.

Main Idea

A young girl's quick thinking saves the life of a very sick child.

Supporting Detail

_____

_____

_____

_____

_____

Supporting Detail

_____

_____

_____

_____

_____

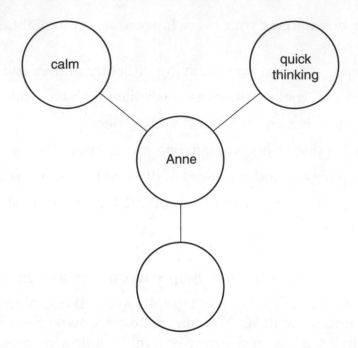

Tip 7 **Use different parts of a book to find information on specific topics.**

Some books will include a table of contents and an index to help you locate information.

Table of contents

The **table of contents** is an outline of a book. Found near the front of a book, it gives a quick look at the main subjects covered and tells the reader where to find those subjects.

Table of Contents	
The History of Video Games	1
How Video Games Are Created	11
Types of Games	36
Becoming a Winner	49
Buying Your Own Video Games	52
Taking Care of Your Video Games	63
Index	72

11. To which page would you turn to find out about the types of video games you could buy?

A. 1

B. 11

C. 36

D. 49

Index

If you want to find information on a specific topic within a book, the **index** is the place to look. It is usually found in the back of a book. The index gives a more detailed list of topics than the table of contents. In fact, the index lists every subject covered in the whole book—in alphabetical order. It also gives you the page numbers where these subjects can be found. Here is part of an index from a book about video games.

Index

A
animation, 12
arcade games, 6, 38, 50
artists. See VIDEO ARTISTS.

B
backgrounds. See SCREEN BACKGROUNDS.
buying games, 52

C
cartridge, 15, 39, 55, 67
circuits, 15
colors, 17
compact discs, 14, 42, 53–54, 66–67
controls, 2, 6, 50, 64

Reading Strategies
Lesson 5 Summary

When answering questions about reading strategies, remember the following tips:

- Be aware of your purpose for reading.

- Look over the passage or book and predict what it will be about.

- Determine what genre (type of writing) you are reading.

- Ask yourself questions as you read and check your understanding.

- From time to time, stop to summarize what you have read.

- Use graphic organizers to help you understand information.

- Use different parts of a book to find information on specific topics.

Practice Passage

Directions: Read the passage, then answer the questions that follow.

Shikaras
by Steve Haney

On the lakes in an area known as the Vale of Kashmir, a fertile Asian mountain valley near the border of India and Pakistan, people get around using a type of boat called a *shikara*.

How They Are Made

Shikaras are made of wood and come in different sizes. They are very long, have flat bottoms, and narrow to a point at both ends. Shikaras look very sleek and graceful. Most are so flat that, from a distance, you can barely see them on the water.

Kinds of Shikaras

There are many kinds of shikaras. Some have little canvas roofs over them to protect passengers from the sun or rain. Some shikaras are simple and plain and unpainted, while others have beautifully carved sides that are painted yellow or blue or pink. The roofs of these more <u>luxurious</u> shikaras have tassels hanging from them, and the big, fancy seats have cushions. Some larger shikaras can carry six or seven people.

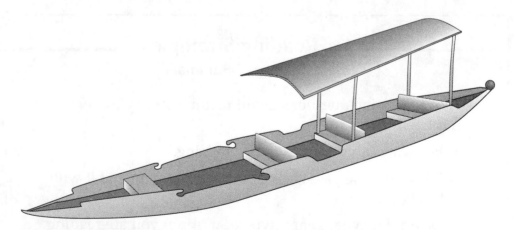

How They Are Propelled

A shikara looks somewhat like a gondola, a type of boat used in Venice, Italy. One difference between the two boats is how they are moved through the water. A shikara driver sits and uses a long paddle. A gondolier stands and uses a long pole to push a gondola.

How They Are Used

Knowing how to paddle a shikara is an important skill, since many families in Kashmir live on houseboats. These houseboats don't move.

They stay in one place on the water, so people must use shikaras to come and go.

If people do not want to leave their houseboats, they can buy what they need from shikara drivers who go from houseboat to houseboat selling goods. Their shikaras are like small, traveling convenience stores.

Imagine an Evening Shikara Ride

Imagine that you are visiting Kashmir. It is evening and you are sitting on the front porch of your houseboat. People stop to talk, or shout greetings to each other as they paddle by. You ask your family if they'd like to take a ride in a shikara.

"I'll drive," you say. ❖

Sample Reading Strategies Questions

1. What kind of genre best describes this passage?
   A. drama
   B. fiction
   C. nonfiction
   D. historical fiction

2. Why would someone want to read this passage?
   A. to find out how to drive a gondola
   B. to gather ideas for a report on Venice
   C. to learn about common transportation in Kashmir
   D. to enjoy a story about a child who lives in a houseboat

3. Which of the following is used by the author to help the reader understand the passage?
   A. maps
   B. graphs
   C. footnotes
   D. section headings

4. In which section of the passage can you find information about how a shikara moves through the water?
   A. How They Are Made
   B. Kinds of Shikaras
   C. How They Are Propelled
   D. How They Are Used

5. Using details from the text, summarize the important information about shikaras.

_____

_____

_____

_____

_____

_____

_____

_____

_____

_____

Additional Practice Questions

6. If you wanted to find out more about the geography of Kashmir, which of the following books would be the best resource?

   A. *Farming Methods in India*

   B. *The Complete Atlas of Asia*

   C. *Webster's New World Dictionary*

   D. *Village Life in Pakistan*

7. In which kind of publication would you most likely find this passage?

   A. a travel brochure about Venice

   B. a website about boating safety

   C. a book about mountains in Asia

   D. a magazine article about Kashmir

8. Which of the following best describes a shikara?
   A. curve-bottomed with a pointed front end
   B. flat-bottomed with a pointed back end
   C. curve-bottomed with a point at both ends
   D. flat-bottomed with a point at each end

9. According to the passage, which of the following is a main difference between gondolas and shikaras?
   A. Gondolas are brightly painted; shikaras are plain and simple.
   B. Gondolas carry five or six people; shikaras carry only two people.
   C. Gondolas are propelled by a pole; shikaras are propelled by a paddle.
   D. Gondolas have hard wooden seats; shikaras have cushioned pillows.

10. As used in the passage, the word *luxurious* means
    A. full of luxury.
    B. without luxury.
    C. gaining luxury.
    D. causing luxury.

11. Which of the following best describes the author's purpose for writing this passage?
    A. to argue
    B. to inform
    C. to entertain
    D. to persuade

12. Why are shikaras so important to many families in Kashmir? Use information from the passage to support your answer.

    _____

    _____

    _____

    _____

    _____

Lesson 6

Made-Up Stories

What's your favorite kind of fiction? Is it a mystery in which someone has to solve a crime? A horror story in which someone tries to get away from a scary monster? A science-fiction story about humans trying to outwit creatures from another galaxy? Or is it a more realistic story—one about family relationships or friendships? Is the story completely made up, or are elements of the story based on history? Maybe your favorite kind of fiction is drama (plays).

There are many different kinds of fiction. But most fictional stories and dramas are based on these three things:

> *a person or persons*
>> *in a place and at a time*
>>> *with a problem*

The people in the story are called the **characters**; however, characters can also be animals, birds, talking trees, sea creatures, and so on. The time and place of the action make up the **setting**. The problems the characters face and the way the problems are solved make up the **plot**.

Most stories follow a set pattern. The *beginning* of a story tells about the characters and the setting. It also tells about the problem or **conflict** faced by the main character or characters.

The *middle*, or *body*, of a story tells how the characters' problem or conflict gets bigger and bigger. The problem or conflict continues to grow until the story reaches its **climax**. The climax is the point in the story where the problem or conflict stops getting bigger and starts to be solved.

The *end* of a story tells how the problem is solved. This is called the story's **resolution**.

Tip 1 **Pay attention to the narrator's point of view. (Who is telling the story?)**

Stories can be told by one of the characters in the story or someone outside the story. The way a plot develops can depend on which technique the author uses.

1. Read the following passage. As you read, underline any words that show you who is telling the story.

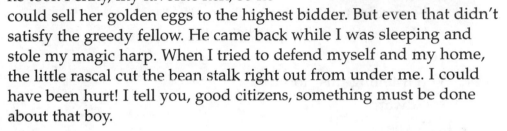

    Something must be done about that boy Jack. It wasn't enough that he almost broke his poor widow mother, selling her best milk cow for a handful of beans. Now he insists on ruining my good name. Calling me "Giant"! How unkind to make fun of someone because of his size. And all that "Fee, fi, fo, fum" stuff. To think that *I*, the very model of gentleness, would go about eating little children!

    Well, let me tell you my side of the story. That boy broke into my house, stole my gold, and ate my supper. Then he took Penny, my favorite hen, so he could sell her golden eggs to the highest bidder. But even that didn't satisfy the greedy fellow. He came back while I was sleeping and stole my magic harp. When I tried to defend myself and my home, the little rascal cut the bean stalk right out from under me. I could have been hurt! I tell you, good citizens, something must be done about that boy.

2. Who is telling this story?
   A. Jack
   B. the giant
   C. Jack's mother
   D. a narrator who is not part of the story

3. How do you know?

   _____

   _____

   _____

   _____

   _____

   _____

Read the following passage by Gertrude Chandler Warner. It is from *The Mystery of the Mixed-Up Zoo*, a book in the Boxcar Children Mysteries series.

As soon as they entered the zoo's gates, they knew something was wrong. Going by the lions, they noticed how restless they were and how they paced back and forth, shaking their manes.

Hurriedly they followed Edward to the Bird House. "Let's see how our tropical friends are doing," Edward said, opening the door.

The macaw screeched, and the green parrot scolded, but on the whole the birds were unusually quiet. Many were hunched over and didn't move.

"Oh," Jessie cried, grabbing her arms, "it's cold in here!"

"I'm cold, too," Benny exclaimed.

"The heat's off!" Edward shouted . . .

4. Who is telling this story?

   A. Edward

   B. Jessie

   C. Benny

   D. a narrator who is not a part of the story

5. How do you know?

   _____

   _____

   _____

   _____

   _____

   _____

Tip 2 **Listen to what the author tells you about the characters.**

Imagine you are describing yourself to a faraway pen pal you've never met. What kinds of things would you tell about yourself? Are you a boy or a girl? What do you look like? What do you like to do? What makes you laugh? What makes you angry or sad?

In a story, the author tells you all sorts of things about the characters. Pay close attention to the words the author uses to tell about each character and what they have to say. Also, think about how the characters are alike or different from each other.

6. Read the following passage from Ann M. Martin's *Kristy and the Worst Kid Ever*, a book from The Baby-Sitters Club series. As you read, underline details that tell you about the characters.

   Mary Anne Spier, the secretary of the BSC [Baby-Sitters Club], is my best friend and although we look alike, with our brown hair and brown eyes, and we're both short, we have totally different personalities. I tend to speak my mind. (Some people would say I have a big mouth. I hate to admit it, but I do say things without thinking sometimes.) Mary Anne, on the other hand, is quiet and shy and sensitive. That doesn't mean you can bully her, though! Although Mary Anne is always willing to see the best in people, she's very perceptive and honest.

Studying the Characters

Here are some questions to ask yourself about the important characters in a story:

- What is each main character like?

- What does each main character want most? Why?

- What is keeping each main character from getting what he or she wants?

- How will the main characters solve their problems?

- Does any main character change during the story? How?

- Ask yourself, "Would this character really do this? Do his or her actions make sense? Why? Why not?"

7. Fill in the diagram below to show details about Mary Anne and
   the narrator (the person telling the story).

	Mary Anne	Narrator
The way they look		
The way they act		

8. In what ways are Mary Anne and the narrator alike?

_____

_____

_____

_____

_____

9. One way in which the narrator is different from Mary Anne is that
   the narrator
   A. is shy.
   B. is short.
   C. has a big mouth.
   D. allows people to bully her.

Tip 3 **Pay attention to the characters' thoughts, words, and actions.**

The things people think, say, and do tell us a lot about the kind of people
they are. Most stories are a mix of words from the storyteller (**narration**) and
the exact thoughts and words of the characters (**dialogue** [DYE-uh-log]).
Exact words that characters say are placed in quotation marks (" ").

Tip 4 **Find out *why* characters do or say the things they do.**

A character's actions and dialogue tell the reader a lot about that character. As you follow a character's actions, ask yourself, "Why is the character doing this? What reasons does the character have for his or her actions?"

Read the following passage and answer Numbers 10 through 14.

Tommy and the Snowballs
by Morris Weaver

Tommy zipped his jacket up to the jawbone and shivered. His mittens were wet, his fingers were numb, and his feet were like two heavy blocks of ice. His efforts in the cold were worth it, though, he thought. "It's payback time!" he said quietly, though no one was there yet to hear. He had made 25 perfect snowballs. Now he waited in the freezing wind for Sparky to come by. He tingled with cold—and with excitement.

In the distance, he could see Sparky's red nylon coat and bright checkered cap moving slowly toward his hideaway. He crouched behind a small cedar hedge, nervously licking his chapped lips and trying to moisten his dry mouth. His heart pounded. His cocked arm was tense and ready.

He squinted, peering through the green branches, timing his first throw carefully. Sparky neared the "strike zone," hands in his pockets, whistling. Tommy froze for an instant, then let the missile fly.

"Bingo! Direct hit, you bully!" he yelled. Tommy grabbed wildly for another snowball. ❖

10. Fill in the diagram below to show details about Tommy.

	Tommy
What he thinks	
What he says	
What he does	

11. Which phrase best describes Tommy?
    A. kind to others
    B. afraid of the cold
    C. longing for friends
    D. not afraid of bullies

12. Based on what you know from the passage, which of the following best describes Sparky?
    A. a bully
    B. an athlete
    C. a friend of Tommy's
    D. a fifth-grade student

13. What does Tommy want to accomplish in this passage?

    _____

    _____

14. Which of the following statements would most likely be made by Tommy?
    A. "You know? That Sparky really is a nice guy."
    B. "Sparky deserves a few well-aimed snowballs."
    C. "Maybe if I ask nicely, Sparky will be my buddy."
    D. "Poor Sparky. I feel bad that he has so few friends."

Tip 5 **Draw conclusions based on details that describe the setting and set the mood.**

Most of the time, an author will give details about the setting—where and when the story takes place. Setting includes what the place looks like. It also includes things like the year, the season, the time of day, and the weather.

The setting sometimes affects the **mood** of the story, or the feeling that the story gives you. The mood of a story can be suspenseful or scary or sad or exciting or funny or . . . well, you get the idea.

15. Read the following passage from *A Wrinkle in Time* by Madeleine L'Engle. As you read, underline words that tell you about the setting of the story.

> It was a dark and stormy night.
> In her attic bedroom Margaret Murry, wrapped in an old patchwork quilt, sat on the foot of her bed and watched the trees tossing in the frenzied lashing of the wind. Behind the trees, clouds scudded[1] frantically across the sky. Every few moments the moon ripped through them, creating wraithlike[2] shadows that raced along the ground.
> The house shook.
> Wrapped in her quilt, Meg shook.
>
> [1] **scudded:** moved quickly
> [2] **wraithlike:** ghostlike

16. Where does the story take place?

   _____

17. When does the story take place?

   _____

18. What is happening at the time of the story?

   _____

19. Which word best describes the mood of the story?
   A. sad   C. funny
   B. scary   D. cheerful

20. Which words in the passage helped you answer Number 19?

   _____

Tip 6 Follow the plot of the story.

The plot is what happens in the story—it's where the action is. The plot is usually based on some problem the characters have.

Read the following passage from *Superfudge* by Judy Blume. At this point in the story, Peter Hatcher has been asked by Mr. Green, the school principal, to help out with Peter's little brother, Fudge. It is Fudge's first day in his kindergarten classroom.

I looked up. Fudge was perched on top of the cabinets that were on top of the cubbies. He was stretched out, lying across the top, just inches from the ceiling.

"Hi, Pee-tah," he called, waving.

"What are you doing up there?" I said.

"Resting."

"Come on down!"

"No. I don't like this school. I quit!"

"You can't quit," Mr. Green said.

"Why not?" Fudge asked.

"Because going to school is your job," Mr. Green said. "Otherwise, what will you be when you grow up?"

"A bird!" Fudge told him.

Mr. Green laughed. "Creative, isn't he?"

21. What is Fudge's main problem in this passage?
    A. He doesn't like school.
    B. He is tired and needs some sleep.
    C. He can't climb down from the cabinets.
    D. He wants to be a bird when he grows up.

22. What problems must Mr. Green and Peter solve?

_____

_____

_____

_____

_____

_____

A character can have many types of problems. Sometimes the character's problem is with a **person**. If you could read on in *Superfudge*, you would find that Fudge has a problem with his teacher, Mrs. Hildebrandt. She wants to call him by his real name, Farley Drexel Hatcher, which he doesn't like one bit.

Sometimes the character's problem is with **nature**. In the first chapter of *Legend of the Lost Legend* by R. L. Stine, Justin and Marissa are lost in Antarctica. One of their biggest problems, besides being lost, is keeping warm.

Sometimes characters have problems within **themselves**. Imagine that your best friend has invited you to a birthday party on the same day that your Scout troop is going on a camping trip. You have to decide which event to attend. The problem—and the solution—is within yourself.

Usually, by the end of the story, the characters will have solved the problem in some way. The way the characters solve the problem often gives you an idea about the theme, or message, the author wants you to get from the story.

Tip 7 **Put together details from the passage to make inferences and draw conclusions.**

Sometimes when authors write stories, they don't fill in every detail. You can make intelligent guesses based on facts from the story and what you know from your own life experience. These guesses based on known facts are called **inferences**, which you will learn more about in Lesson 9.

For example, go back to the passage from *Superfudge*.

23. What does Mr. Green do when Fudge says he wants to be a bird?

_____

_____

_____

_____

24. Based on Mr. Green's reaction to Fudge's behavior, how do you think Mr. Green gets along with young people?

_____

_____

_____

_____

Tip 8 **Make predictions about what will happen next in the story.**

The things you learn about a story's plot can also help you predict what will happen next in the story. As the story continues, you will find out how all the problems are solved. Read the passage from *Superfudge* again. Then answer Numbers 25 and 26.

25. What is most likely to happen next in the story?
    A. Fudge will go home and not come back.
    B. Mr. Green will release Fudge from kindergarten.
    C. Fudge will take a long nap on top of the cabinet.
    D. Peter and Mr. Green will talk Fudge into coming down.

When making predictions, be sure to base your answers on information in the passage. Wild predictions aren't usually very likely ones. Something from the passage should support your answer.

26. What details support your prediction in Number 25?

_____

_____

_____

_____

_____

_____

Tip 9 **Use a story map to keep track of the characters, setting, and plot.**

Making a **story map** is one way you can keep track of the important parts of a story.

27. Complete the story map below for the passage from *Superfudge*.
    (Since we aren't told the solution in this passage, make a prediction
    about how the problem will be solved.)

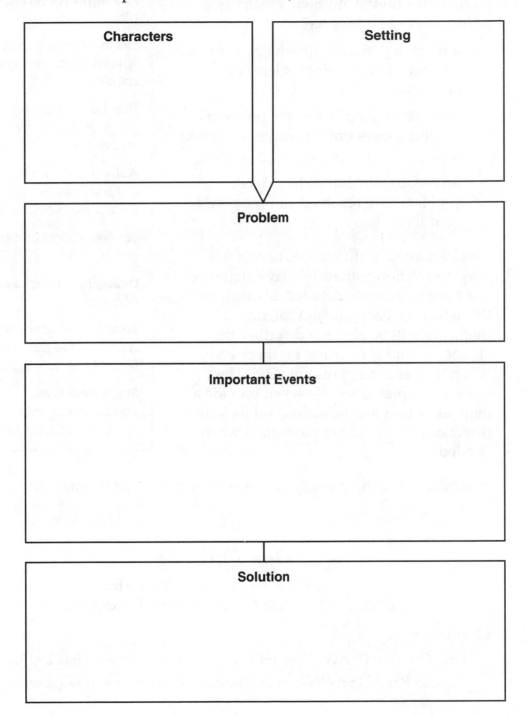

Tip 10 Most plays follow the same pattern (or form) as a work of fiction.

Drama, like fiction, involves *characters*, *setting*, and *plot*. Plays have

- a *beginning*, which introduces us to the characters and their problems or conflicts;

- a *middle*, during which the problem or conflict grows until it reaches a climax; and

- an *end*, in which the characters' problems are resolved and the play's conflict ends.

One of the major differences between a play and fiction is that the playwright does not have to provide detailed descriptions of the setting or characters. Audience members will be able to "describe" the characters and the setting for themselves when they see the play produced. The author of a play does, however, provide a general setting for the action and include directions for character movement when needed.

Drama Terms
Playwright – the author of a play
Stage – a platform upon which actors move and speak
Theatre – a building with a stage and seats for the audience
Act – a part of a play (Each act is usually made up of smaller parts called scenes.)
Scene – a part of a play's act
Dialogue – the spoken words of a play
Setting – the scenery used in a play, or the place and time of the action
Stage Directions – instructions for movement, lighting, music, and so on

Read the following passage and answer Numbers 28 through 31.

from

Don Quixote

by Miguel de Cervantes Saavedra
adapted and written for the stage by Gordon Mertz

Characters:

Don Quixote (DAWN kee-HO-tay)—an old man who has lost his wits
Sancho Panza (SAWN-cho PON-zuh)—Quixote's squire (servant)
Innkeeper

ACT ONE
Scene 2

(*Scene: A crude, dingy country inn with attached stable*)

*(Enter **Quixote** in rusted and ill-fitting armor, accompanied by **Panza**. The two men are in heated debate. The **innkeeper** observes them with amazement.)*

Panza: But master, your armor is rusted through and the face plate on your helmet will not stay up—and look, master, you've lost one of your spurs.

Quixote: *(Ignoring **Panza**)* Why are there no trumpets? You, keeper of this castle, do you not recognize me? I am Don Quixote de la Mancha, glorious defender of this land and all who dwell in it. Is it too much to ask for a trumpet flourish upon my arrival?

Innkeeper: *(Astonished)* Trumpet flourish? Keeper of the castle? Are you mad, sir?

Panza: He's quite mad, sir, but also quite noble.

Quixote: *(To the **innkeeper**)* Pay no attention to my knave, sir. *(The sound of pigs squealing is heard from the stable)* At last, my trumpet flourish. And now, to our feast.

Innkeeper: Feast indeed! Remove your helmet, grandfather, and follow me.

Quixote: I am unable to remove the helmet due to its misshapen form. I will wear it to dine and wear it to sleep. I shall not remove it until I have righted the wrongs of this world.

Innkeeper: As you wish. *(Seats the two men, grabs a loaf of bread and tosses it onto the table)* Your feast, my lords.

Quixote: Magnificent! Compliment the chefs of your kitchens! Sancho, we dine in splendor this night.

Panza: *(Aside)* We choke down moldy bread is more like it.

*(**Quixote** tries to eat the bread but his helmet visor continues to fall, knocking it out of his hand. Disgusted, he rises abruptly from the table and drops to his knees in front of a startled **innkeeper**.)*

Quixote: I shall not rise until your worship dubs me Knight of La Mancha. Such action will bring you great praise and benefit all of mankind.

Innkeeper: *(Tapping **Quixote** on the shoulder with the flat side of a meat cleaver and reading in a monotone from his account book)* Leg of mutton, 20 peseta; ale, 60 peseta; oats, 80 peseta; hay, 12 peseta; bread, 4 peseta. I now dub you Don Quixote de La Mancha. Please pay in advance if you want a room.

(The pigs squeal again.)

Quixote: *(Rising)* Thank you, your worship, for the fine ceremony, and thank your trumpeters for the flourish. I am now at the service of the masses. *(Raising his visor and sitting again at the table)* And now, your worship, a dish of butter for Sancho and me—*(The visor drops again)* and a candle, if you please.

(Curtain)

28. Which of the following best describes Sancho Panza?
    A. fearless
    B. patient
    C. elegant
    D. discouraged

29. The author gives movements and instructions to the actor by using
    A. parentheses with <u>underlined type</u>.
    B. parentheses with CAPITALS.
    C. parentheses with regular type.
    D. parentheses with *italic* and ***bold italic*** type.

30. How does the innkeeper react to Quixote's odd behavior by the end of this scene?
    A. He becomes angry with Quixote's demands.
    B. He realizes that Quixote is an honored nobleman.
    C. He ignores Quixote and tries to get Sancho to pay for a room.
    D. He accepts Quixote's craziness and goes along with his requests.

31. What does Quixote confuse as a "trumpet flourish"?
    A. squealing pigs
    B. moldy bread
    C. a rusty helmet
    D. a meat cleaver

Made-Up Stories
Lesson 6 Summary

When answering questions about parts of a story, remember the following tips:

- Pay attention to the narrator's point of view. (Who is telling the story?)
- Listen to what the author tells you about the characters.
- Pay attention to the characters' thoughts, words, and actions.
- Find out *why* characters do or say the things they do.
- Draw conclusions based on details that describe the setting and set the mood.
- Follow the plot of the story.
- Put together details from the passage to make inferences and draw conclusions.
- Make predictions about what will happen next in the story.
- Use a story map to keep track of characters, setting, and plot.
- Most plays follow the same pattern (or form) as a work of fiction.

Practice Passage

Directions: Read the passage, then answer the questions that follow.

from

I Left My Sneakers in Dimension X
by Bruce Coville

When Rod Allbright finds out that his less-than-favorite cousin Elspeth is coming to visit for two weeks during summer vacation, he is not too happy. Little does he know that Elspeth's visit will be much more exciting—and frightening— than either of them could have guessed. Read on to find out what happens when Rod, Elspeth, and Rod's dog, Bonehead, go for a walk in the field behind the Allbrights' house.

Elspeth's <u>nonstop</u> chatter—combined with her need to point out every flaw in my face, body, clothing, and room—was driving me berserk.

"I think I'll take Bonehead out to Seldom Seen for a while," I said to my mother, after breakfast.

Seldom Seen is what we call the field behind our house. We live out in the country, and our backyard slopes down to a swamp thick with big old willow trees. On the far side of the swamp, surrounded by woods, is a big field where Grampa still grows corn. He named it "Seldom Seen" because—well, because it's seldom seen. You can only get to it by crossing the swamp on a little wooden bridge my father and some of his friends built, or by going through a neighbor's automobile junkyard.

It is a very private place, and I love it out there. I had intended to go on my own. So you can imagine how pleased I was when my mother said, "That's a good idea, Rod. Why don't you take Elspeth along?"

I sighed. It wasn't even worth fighting about. I knew I would lose. At least she didn't make me take the twins. (This was just as well, considering what was waiting for me out there.)

I started to put on my new sneakers, which were sort of a bribe from Mom for putting up with Elspeth, and got ready to leave.

"Do you think you should wear those, Rod?" asked Mom—meaning, of course, that *she* didn't think I should wear them. They were expensive, and I knew she had to stretch the budget to buy them. But what was the use of sneakers if you couldn't wear them? Even so, I might have changed my mind, if Elspeth hadn't <u>chimed in</u>.

"Your mother's right," she said primly. "You'll probably get them all muddy crossing the swamp."

I grunted and continued tying my laces. Mom sighed and turned away. I felt bad, but not bad enough to take off the sneakers.

With Elspeth bouncing along behind me, and Bonehead bouncing along behind her, I headed for the swamp.

I figured things couldn't get worse, until we actually made it to Seldom Seen and stumbled into a hole. It was enormous—about a foot deep and nearly twenty feet long. I knew it would upset my grandfather, because whatever had made it had mashed down the young corn stalks.

Then I realized what the hole really was. I stopped worrying about what my grandfather would think and concentrated on staying calm. It wasn't easy. My heart pounding with terror, I whispered, "Let's get out of here, Elspeth."

"Why? I like it back here."

"Don't you see what this is?" I asked.

She made a face. "Yeah, it's a hole in the ground. So what?"

I swallowed, then pointed to the front of the hole, yards away, where I could see four distinct marks.

Toe marks.

"This isn't just a *hole*," I hissed. "We're standing in a footprint!" ❖

Sample Story Elements Questions

1. Which word would Rod most likely use to describe Elspeth?
   A. shy
   B. helpful
   C. friendly
   D. annoying

2. Which of the following best describes "Seldom Seen"?
   A. a cornfield surrounded by woods
   B. a neighbor's junkyard next to a swamp
   C. a swamp thick with big old willow trees
   D. a wooded area that slopes down from Rod's backyard

3. What is Rod's main problem at the beginning of the story?
   A. He finds a giant footprint at Seldom Seen.
   B. His cousin Elspeth is driving him crazy.
   C. His mom wants him to take the twins to Seldom Seen.
   D. His mom doesn't want him to wear his new sneakers.

4. Why doesn't Rod openly disagree with his mother about taking Elspeth with him to Seldom Seen?

_____

_____

_____

_____

_____

_____

5. From reading the passage, you can tell that Rod doesn't want to take off his new sneakers because

    A. he wants to impress Elspeth.

    B. he wants to make his mother angry.

    C. Elspeth tells him not to wear them.

    D. his other shoes are old and falling apart.

6. Which sentence best completes this diagram of the story's plot?

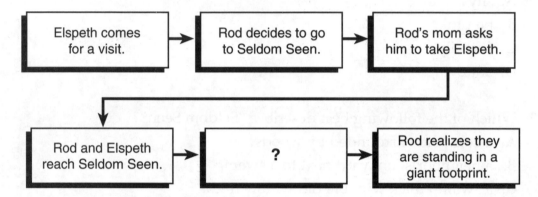

    A. Elspeth drives Rod "berserk."

    B. Rod puts on his new sneakers.

    C. Elspeth and Rod stumble into a giant hole.

    D. Rod and Elspeth cross the bridge over a swamp.

7. Which sentence best describes how Rod feels about Elspeth?

    A. He dislikes her.

    B. He is afraid of her.

    C. He is jealous of her.

    D. He enjoys her company.

8. Who is telling this story?

    A. Rod

    B. Elspeth

    C. Rod's mom

    D. a narrator who is not part of the story

Additional Practice Questions

9. As it is used in this story, what does the word *nonstop* mean?
   A. full of stops
   B. never starting
   C. without stopping
   D. starting and stopping

10. Read the following sentence from paragraph 4.

   So you can imagine how pleased I was when my mother said, "That's a good idea, Rod. Why don't you take Elspeth along?"

   What does Rod actually mean when he says, "So you can imagine how pleased I was . . ."?
   A. He wants to take Elspeth with him.
   B. He wants his mother to use her imagination.
   C. He is not happy about taking Elspeth with him.
   D. He is not really planning to let Elspeth go with him.

11. What effect does the author create with the following sentence from paragraph 5?

   "This was just as well, considering what was waiting for me out there."

   A. He shows Rod's concern for his mother and Elspeth.
   B. He develops a mood of despair and sadness in the story.
   C. He shows Rod's unhappiness about taking his cousin Elspeth with him.
   D. He creates suspense by hinting that something bad is about to happen.

12. As it is used in this story, the words *chimed in* most likely mean
   A. rang.
   B. threw.
   C. broke.
   D. commented.

13. What is the author's purpose in writing this story?
   A. to teach
   B. to entertain
   C. to inform
   D. to persuade

Lesson 7

Words That Sing

Poetry is different from any other kind of writing.

A poem's words send the reader a message. Poets send their messages by using special words and by placing their lines on the page in special ways. Most poems are written to tell about normal, everyday things or feelings in new and unusual ways.

The following are some tips for reading and enjoying poetry and figurative language.

Tip 1 **Read the poem from beginning to end to get the main idea.**

Poems tell stories or help us think about things in new ways. Most poems are easy to read. When you read a poem for the first time, don't get hung up on little details or on a single line that you might not understand. Just as when you read a story, ask yourself, "What is this *mainly* about?"

Falling Star
by Tiffany Carlisle

Alone, with all the world in bed,
I watched a star burn blue and red.
It streaked across the midnight skies
Like fifty thousand fireflies.
Then, poof! the sparkling flame went dead.
I crawled in darkness to my bed.

1. What do you think this poem is about?

_____

_____

_____

Tip 2 **Go back and read the poem again, this time more slowly.**

A poet tries to say a lot with very few words. He or she wants to make each word count. To fully understand and enjoy a poem, look closely at what the poet is saying in each line. Also pay attention to how he or she is saying it.

Tip 3 **Some poems rhyme and some don't.**

Poets sometimes end lines with rhyming words that have the same vowel sounds and the same final consonants (cat/hat; candy/handy). Some poems are less structured without a set pattern of rhyming words.

2. Does the poet of "Falling Star" use rhyming words? Explain your answer using examples from the poem.

_____

_____

_____

Tip 4 **Writers compare things using similes and metaphors.**

Writers—especially poets—go to a lot of trouble to find fresh ways of saying and showing things. A writer has many ways to paint pictures with words. In this lesson, you will learn about a few of the methods they use.

Similes compare two things by using the words *like* or *as*.

Freddie is growing **like** *a weed.*

Superman is **as fast as** *a speeding bullet.*

Read the passage and answer Numbers 3 and 4.

Football and the Wild, Wild West
by Tom Fitzpatrick

In some ways, football has replaced the Wild West. The football player is like the cowboy of an earlier age, testing his skills and courage, proving he can survive in a dangerous world. He roams the playing field as a cowboy would roam the wide-open prairie. Tackling an opponent is like wrestling down a steer. Returning a kick is like riding into a stampede. Throwing a football is like throwing a lasso—success depends on good aim. ❖

3. Underline all examples of simile in the previous passage.

4. What is the main comparison the author makes using similes?

_____

_____

_____

Metaphors compare two things by describing one thing in terms of another. When authors use metaphors, they don't say one thing is *like* another; they say one thing *is* another.

> America is a melting pot.
> *(America is compared to a melting pot.)*

> Roslyn swam through an ocean of homework.
> *(Homework is compared to an ocean.)*

> Diamonds twinkled in the night sky.
> *(Stars are compared to diamonds.)*

Read the poem and answer Numbers 5 and 6.

Ships

by Mickey Toom

The white clouds are tall clipper ships
With sails filled and billowed.
I watch their prows as each ship plows
Through sky-seas, softly pillowed.

The black clouds are bold pirate ships
On dark horizons looming.
I hear the crash and see the flash
Of their great cannons booming.

5. Find at least two lines in the poem that contain metaphors. Underline them.

6. What is the poet actually describing when he uses the metaphor, *I hear the crash and see the flash/Of their great cannons booming*?

   A. cannons firing

   B. airplanes flying

   C. ships' engines roaring

   D. thunder and lightning

Tip 5 **Writers stress ideas with exaggeration and repetition.**

Writers sometimes go beyond the truth by using **exaggeration** to stress meaning. A writer may be trying to make an important point or simply trying to get a laugh. Another word for exaggeration is **hyperbole** (hi-PER-buh-lee). Here's an example:

> *All the chocolate in Hershey, Pennsylvania, wouldn't be enough for Charlotte.*

Read the poem and answer Numbers 7 and 8.

from

Going Too Far

by Mildred Howells

A woman who lived in Holland of old,
Polished her brass till it shone like gold.
She washed her pig after all its meals
In spite of his energetic squeals.
She scrubbed her doorstep into the ground,
And the children's faces, pink and round,
She washed so hard that in several cases
She polished the features off their faces. . . .

7. Underline any examples of hyperbole (exaggeration) in the poem.

8. Do you think the poet's use of hyperbole makes this poem serious or funny? Explain your answer.

_____

_____

_____

Poets also can stress meaning by repeating words. This is called **repetition**. Most songs use repetition, too. Whenever you sing the chorus of a song, you are using repetition because you are repeating the same words over and over.

9. What song do you know that uses repetition?

_____

Read the poem and answer Numbers 10 and 11.

from

A Very Little Sphinx

by Edna St. Vincent Millay

Wonder where this horseshoe went.
Up and down, up and down,
Up and past the monument,
Maybe into town.

10. What words are repeated in the poem?

_____

11. The repeated words in this poem help the poet show which of the following?
    A. size of the horse
    B. shape of the horseshoe
    C. sound of the horse's hooves
    D. distance to reach the monument

Tip 6 **Writers use personification to make nonhuman things seem human.**

Sometimes an author gives an animal or object human qualities, making it "person-like." This is called **personification**.

Dad screamed as the copy machine ate page after page.

The moon looked down upon a quiet countryside.

A copy machine may tear and crumple pages, but it doesn't actually "eat" paper, and the moon is not actually able to "look down upon" anything, as a person might.

In the following lines, springtime is described as a woman. Read the excerpt and then complete Number 12.

from

Springtime

by Juanita Kopaska

Her sighs bring breezes, warm and sweet;
Green grasses grow beneath her feet.
Lush apple blossoms crown her head—
As tulips curtsy from their bed.

12. Underline any words in the poem that show a human likeness (personification).

Tip 7 **Writers use words that excite the senses.**

Sensory words describe something we can taste, feel, hear, smell, or see. Authors use sensory words to create images we can sense. Here are some examples:

Taste	The ocean spray was as salty as a teardrop.
Touch	Gina tensed as the cold snake slithered across her bare foot.
Sound	The old truck coughed and wheezed its way up the hill.
Smell	The freshly washed laundry smelled of rose petals.
Sight	The diamond sparkled like sunlight on the sea.

Read the passage and answer Number 13.

Marvin's Mystery Soup

The spicy scent of Marvin's mystery soup filled the house. I peeked into the kitchen and saw the brown liquid oozing from under the lid. It sizzled as it slid down the sides of the huge pot and hit the burner. I walked over, lifted the heavy lid, and felt the rising steam against my face. I looked inside, not believing what I saw—floating bits of black and green, and every now and then, something that looked like a sock.

13. Underline the sensory words in the passage above.

Words That Sing

Lesson 7 Summary

When answering poetry and figurative language questions, remember the following tips:

- Read the poem from beginning to end to get the main idea.

- Go back and read the poem again, this time more slowly.

- Some poems rhyme and some don't.

- Writers compare things using similes and metaphors.

- Writers stress ideas with exaggeration and repetition.

- Writers use personification to make nonhuman things seem human.

- Writers use words that excite the senses.

Practice Passage

Directions: Read the poem, then answer the questions that follow.

Night Flight

by Mike Acton

I built a box kite with my dad
One Saturday
In March.
Its frame was made of balsa wood;
Its surface, sheets of yellow silk.

It was a thing of glory in the sky—
As proud as springtime sunlight,
And as high as swallows fly.

I kept it up all afternoon
And just at dusk I hauled it in.
Dad taped a tiny penlight
To the wooden spars,
And as the night breeze hummed,
I sent it up again.

It rode against a blue-black sky,
With silken hull a glow of yellow light
That must have startled dim-lit stars.

It swung high in the windy dark,
A yellow lantern lost at sea,
And talked to me
Down paths invisible—
Along a <u>taut</u> and singing string.

Sample Poetry Questions

1. Summarize the poem in your own words.

_____

_____

_____

_____

_____

_____

_____

2. Which of the following lines provides an example of simile?
   A. I built a box kite with my dad
   B. Its frame was made of balsa wood
   C. As proud as springtime sunlight
   D. It swung high in the windy dark

3. The poet compares how high the kite is flying to
   A. sheets of yellow silk.
   B. swallows in the sky.
   C. the glow of yellow light.
   D. the windy dark.

4. Which of the following lines does the poet use to help the reader hear the wind?

    A. I kept it up all afternoon

    B. To the wooden spars

    C. And as the night breeze hummed

    D. With silken hull a glow of yellow light

5. Which of the following lines provides an example of personification?

    A. And just at dusk I hauled it in

    B. I sent it up again

    C. It rode against a blue-black sky

    D. Along a taut and singing string

6. What is the poet describing with the metaphor "A yellow lantern lost at sea"?

_____

_____

_____

_____

_____

Additional Practice Questions

7. In the last line of the poem, what does the word *taut* mean?

    A. soft   C. cloth

    B. tight   D. schooled

8. The poet most likely wrote "Night Flight" to

    A. explain how kites are made.

    B. convince readers to buy kites.

    C. teach readers how to fly a kite at night.

    D. entertain readers with a story about flying a kite.

9. Who is the speaker in this poem?

    A. a child   C. a kite

    B. a dad   D. a speaker outside the poem

Real People, Events, and Information

There are many kinds of **nonfiction** writing. In fact, anything you read that is not a made-up story is nonfiction. Although newspapers, textbooks, instruction manuals, almanacs, encyclopedias, and other reference materials are all types of nonfiction, the term is normally applied to true stories such as magazine articles or essays that deal with *real subjects—real people and real events*.

Tip 1 **Authors organize nonfiction materials in many ways.**

Nonfiction can be organized in many different ways, including these common approaches:

- **sequence of events** (the author describes events in the order they happen or by listing instructional steps in the order they should be followed)

- **cause and effect** (the author describes how one event or condition affects another)

- **compare and contrast** (the author shows how two or more events are alike and different)

- **detailed description** (the author provides detailed facts, figures, and other information about the topic)

- **problem/solution** (the author presents a problem and its solution, then moves on to another problem)

- **order of importance** (the author presents facts and details from most important to least important or vice versa)

Authors organize their materials in a certain order to help the reader follow their ideas more easily. But remember, they may choose to combine these types of organization. For example, an author may tell about events in the order they happened and at the same time describe the cause of each event and the effect it had on following events.

Tip 2 **Many nonfiction books and articles are written to give information.**

Informational writing gives facts and details about real things. It does not tell a story. Read the following nonfiction article.

Hang on for the Ride!

by Jim Bartlett

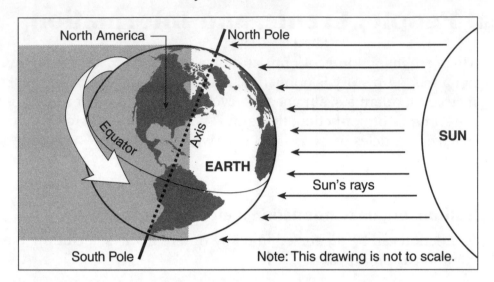

Although you might feel as if you are firmly planted in one place, you are moving every second of your life. You can't feel it, but each day you move thousands of miles through space.

The Earth actually has two kinds of motion: rotation and revolution. To understand rotation, imagine a line from the North Pole to the South Pole through the center of the Earth. This line is called the Earth's axis. The Earth rotates, or spins, on its axis once every 24 hours. To picture this spinning motion, think about a basketball spinning on the tip of a person's finger very slowly.

As the Earth spins one full turn, we experience day and night. So, when Ohio faces the Sun, it is daytime here and nighttime in China—on the opposite side of the world. When Ohio is turned away from the Sun, it is nighttime here and daytime in China. Day after day, the Earth's rotation never stops. This also is true for the other planets, which spin just as the Earth does.

At the same time, our spinning planet travels in a long loop around the Sun. The Earth makes one revolution (trip around the Sun) each year. To understand revolution, think about a merry-go-round. Imagine that the center of the merry-go-round is the Sun. Now imagine that you are the Earth, sitting on a merry-go-round horse, circling around the Sun. The other horses on the merry-go-round are the other planets, some closer to the Sun than you are, some farther away. Unlike a merry-go-round, however, the planets orbit (revolve around) the Sun at different speeds and none of them follow the same path.

So, if you can't sit still, don't worry. No one is sitting still, night or day. We're all on a wonderful high-speed ride around the solar system. Hang on! ❖

Answer the following questions, which are the types of items you will often see with an informational passage.

1. The main purpose of the diagram is to show the Earth's
   A. rotation on its axis.
   B. distance from the Sun.
   C. revolution around the Sun.
   D. orbit compared to other planets.

2. Which of the following ideas best completes the chart?

```
          ┌───────────────────┐
          │ Earth's Movements │
          └───────────────────┘
           ╱                 ╲
┌─────────────────┐   ┌─────────────────┐
│ Rotation        │   │ Revolution      │
│ • Earth spins   │   │ • Earth travels │
│   on its axis   │   │   around the    │
│ • One rotation  │   │   Sun           │
│   completed     │   │ • ?             │
│   each day      │   │                 │
└─────────────────┘   └─────────────────┘
```

   A. different distances from the Sun
   B. one revolution completed each year
   C. one revolution completed each day
   D. a line from the top of the Earth to the bottom

3. What is the main idea of this passage?
   A. The Earth spins on its axis.
   B. The Earth is always in motion.
   C. The Earth revolves around the Sun.
   D. Ohio has day while China has night.

4. In the diagram, most of North America is experiencing
   A. sunrise.
   B. sunset.
   C. darkness.
   D. daylight.

Tip 3 Know what kinds of learning resources are available to you.

When you read to learn about a subject, it's important to use different sources of information. By using more than one source, you'll be able to compare important details about the subject and make sure your sources are accurate (correct). The following are some sources of information other than nonfiction books.

Magazines

Magazines contain articles about all sorts of things. Some magazines, such as *Time* and *Newsweek*, focus on a variety of topics in the news. Others focus on such topics as sports, fashion, foods, hobbies, business, computers, and history. The list goes on and on! Although many magazine articles are true stories, some magazines contain fictional stories, as well.

Many magazines, such as *People*, are published weekly. Others, such as *Reader's Digest*, are published only once a month. Magazines are published less frequently than most newspapers.

5. What magazine or magazines have you read?

_____

_____

_____

Newspapers

Most **newspapers**, such as the *Columbus Dispatch* or the *Dayton News*, are printed daily. Some small-town newspapers, such as the *Tipp City Herald* and the *New Carlisle Sun*, are printed only once a week. Newspapers contain articles about important day-to-day events. The articles may be about local events or events around the globe. The information in a newspaper is usually more current than information in a magazine.

6. What is the name of a newspaper sold in your hometown?

_____

Online resources

In addition to providing books, newspapers, magazines, and so on, many school libraries and media centers are connected to the **Internet**. Such connections allow you to go online to find information on nearly any topic.

Tip 4 **Decide which type of resource connects to your topic.**

Imagine that you have just read an article about Amelia Earhart, an American pilot. The article tells that, in 1932, Earhart became the first woman to fly solo

---

Use Accurate and Current Resources

Here's a list that will help you determine the value of your resources.

• Where was the information found? (Was the material published in a respected magazine or on a cereal box?)

• What is the author's purpose?

• What makes the author an expert?

• Where does the author get his or her information? (Check to see if the author lists sources. Are his or her resources current and accurate?)

• Are there links to other good sources?

• Be sure to use more than one source of information.

across the Atlantic Ocean. When she attempted to fly around the world, her plane mysteriously disappeared. Amelia Earhart was never seen again. You want to find out more about her life, but where should you look?

Think about what kind of information is usually included in different resources. Then decide which resource would most likely include the information that you're looking for. Try this out on Number 7.

7. If you wanted additional information about Amelia Earhart, which source would help most?

    A. a website that sells toy airplanes

    B. an atlas titled *Maps of the World's Oceans*

    C. the *Illustrated Encyclopedia of Aircraft*

    D. a book titled *Famous American Pilots: Their Lives and Legends*

You are looking for information about Amelia Earhart's life. Choice D is clearly the best source to find out more. A website that sells toy airplanes (choice A) might have a plane that looks like the one Earhart piloted, but probably wouldn't have any other information about her. A book of maps (choice B) wouldn't give any information about Earhart, except you could see where she was flying when she disappeared. Choice C is an encyclopedia with pictures of aircraft, which wouldn't be that helpful in learning more about Earhart's life.

Tip 5 **Some informational materials, such as directions or instructions, are written to help you accomplish a task or do a job.**

An important part of reading is being able to apply what you read to a variety of situations. If the knowledge you gain from reading can't be used, or is used incorrectly, then you are not getting much from what you learn.

The following steps will help you get through any set of instructions so you can apply the information to the task at hand.

- Read instructions from beginning to end before you begin working on the steps.

- Make sure instructions are clear and complete before you begin. Identify any information that is confusing or unnecessary to accomplish the task.

- Collect all materials needed to follow the instructions.

- Follow the instructions in order, without skipping any steps.

- Pay close attention to the diagrams or pictures that go with the instructions. Use them to guide you through the steps.

Read the following owner's manual, then answer Numbers 8 through 12.

Easy-to-Use™ Microwave Oven Owner's Manual

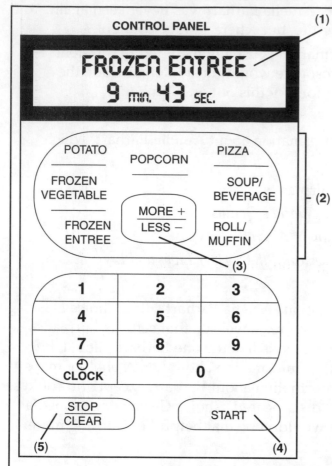

1. **Display window**

   Shows cooking time in minutes and seconds during cooking. Shows clock time when oven is not in use.

2. **Direct-Access menu keypads**

   (See *"Easy-to-Use* Cooking/Heating," below.)

3. **MORE/LESS keypad**

   Adds or reduces cooking time for Direct-Access menu keypads.

4. **START keypad**

5. **STOP/CLEAR keypad**

   • Clears previous setting if pressed before cooking starts.

   • To stop oven during cooking, press once.

   • To stop and clear all entries, press twice.

Beep sound

A beep tone sounds when a keypad on the control panel is touched to indicate a setting has been entered.

Easy-to-Use Cooking/Heating

The seven Direct-Access menu keypads allow for quick and easy cooking/heating of selected categories of food.

Follow the chart at the right, and press the appropriate keypad one to three times (depending on servings/weights). Then press **START**.

Direct-Access menu keypad	once	twice	3 times
SOUP/BEVERAGE	1 serving	2 servings	3 servings
ROLL/MUFFIN	1 serving	2 servings	3 servings
PIZZA	1 serving	2 servings	3 servings
POTATO	1 potato	2 potatoes	3 potatoes
FROZEN VEGETABLE	5 oz.	10 oz.	16 oz.
FROZEN ENTREE	6 oz.	9 oz.	20 oz.
POPCORN	1.75 oz.	3.0 oz.	3.5 oz.

Example: To heat 2 servings of soup:

(SOUP/ BEVERAGE) (MORE + / LESS −) (START)

1. Press **Soup/ Beverage** twice.

2. If desired, press **More/Less** once or twice to adjust cooking time.

3. Press **Start**. Heating starts and time counts down in display.

Note: Consumer information, comments, questions, contact:
Southwest Electronics, Microwave Division
340 Zap Road
Tucson, Arizona 85726

8. How many Direct-Access menu keypads are available on this microwave?

   A. 3

   B. 5

   C. 7

   D. 9

9. What should you do first if you want to microwave soup using the Direct-Access menu keypads?

   A. listen for the beep sound

   B. check the display window

   C. press the SOUP/BEVERAGE keypad

   D. decide how many servings you are microwaving

10. The Direct-Access menu keypad lists only a limited number of food categories. For which food item would you need to select your own cooking time?

    A. cocoa

    B. muffins

    C. apple pie

    D. frozen peas

11. If you make a mistake while choosing your selection, which keypad will clear the incorrect selection?

    A. the (CLOCK) button

    B. the (START) keypad

    C. the (STOP/CLEAR) keypad

    D. the (MORE + / LESS –) keypad

12. What information is missing that would be helpful to the microwave owner?

    A. how to set the clock timer

    B. how to cook three potatoes

    C. how to use the (STOP/CLEAR) keypad

    D. how to contact Southwest Electronics Microwave Division

Tip 6 **Biographies and autobiographies tell true stories about people's lives.**

Authors often use two special kinds of writing called biography and autobiography to tell true stories about a real person's life. Although these genres tell life stories in different ways, they have many things in common.

An **autobiography** is a true story about the writer's life. Anyone can write his or her own autobiography. Writers of autobiographies are writing about themselves. Autobiography writers use words such as *I, me, we, mine,* or *our*.

13. If you were to write an autobiography, what would you title your book?

A **biography** is a nonfiction story about a person's life written by another person. People who write biographies aren't talking about themselves. They're talking about someone else. If you wrote about the life of George Washington, your grandmother, or any real person except yourself, your story would be a biography.

Biographers tell about the main character using words such as *she, her, he, him, his, they, their,* and the character's name.

Look at the following information about a biography. Use it to answer Number 14.

The Life of Thomas Jefferson by Amy Sheldon and Alan Hoskinson, illustrated by Loras Scheuller

14. This book is a biography about
    A. Amy Sheldon.
    B. Loras Scheuller.
    C. Alan Hoskinson.
    D. Thomas Jefferson.

15. Which of the following books is a biography?
    A. *Story of My Life* by Moshe Dayan
    B. *My Indian Boyhood* by Luther Standing Bear
    C. *My Life for the Poor* by Mother Teresa of Calcutta
    D. *The Life and Adventures of Daniel Boone* by Erwin Panofsky

Read the passage and answer Numbers 16 through 21.

John Hockenberry: A Man of Action
by Tom Fitzpatrick

Veteran newsman John Hockenberry joined *Dateline NBC* as a correspondent in January 1996 after a fifteen-year career in broadcast news at both National Public Radio and ABC.

Over the years, John has received many honors, including two Peabody Awards for distinguished broadcasting. As a radio and television reporter, John has traveled all over the world. He has visited Kosovar refugee camps in Albania, interviewed government leaders in Russia, and covered battles in Israel and the Middle East. He loves the challenge of going to dangerous places where few dare to travel. And no matter where his work takes him or how he travels—by jet, by Jeep, by donkey—John completes at least part of his journey in a wheelchair.

This globe-traveling correspondent has been without the use of his legs for more than 20 years, since being injured in an automobile accident as a teenager.

If you were to listen to the story of John's life, it would sound like an adventure novel. It is a mixture of many exciting details about his news-gathering journeys around the world. It is also the story of his day-to-day struggle to live an active life while confined to a wheelchair.

And John's life has been active, indeed. For example, in 1985, he finished the Chicago Marathon in 2 hours and 38 minutes. In 1989, he covered the Middle East for National Public Radio. Rattling and bouncing through the ancient, cobbled streets of Jerusalem, he became known as "The Journalist of the Wheelchair." In 1991, gas mask in hand, he covered frightening and dangerous missile attacks during the Gulf War.

John Hockenberry is a man of action, a man of bravery, and a man of keen observation. But mostly, John Hockenberry is a man who refuses to let physical challenges keep him from making contributions to his nation and the world in which he lives. ❖

16. This passage is an example of which genre?
    A. fiction   C. autobiography
    B. biography   D. instructional text

17. Which of the following best describes the author's purpose for writing this passage?
    A. to entertain people with enjoyable stories
    B. to persuade people to visit the Middle East
    C. to inform people about a remarkable person
    D. to teach the reader how to become a news correspondent

18. How does the author organize the information in this passage?

    A. He lists Hockenberry's accomplishments from most important to least important.

    B. He gives a mix of facts about Hockenberry's life that have taken place over the past 20 years.

    C. He discusses each award Hockenberry has won over the years, starting with the most recent.

    D. He presents Hockenberry's problems in life and tells about how those problems were solved.

19. If John Hockenberry were asked to fly on the space shuttle, he would probably

    A. say no because of the dangers involved.

    B. say no because of his physical limitations.

    C. accept so he could get his name in the news.

    D. accept so he could succeed at one more challenge.

20. The author compares John Hockenberry's life to an adventure novel because

    A. he covered dangerous missile attacks.

    B. he won many awards for his adventure novels.

    C. he lives an exciting life as a journalist and a man of action.

    D. he finished the Chicago Marathon in 2 hours and 38 minutes.

21. What advice would John Hockenberry most likely give to someone facing a physical disability?

    A. Become a journalist so you can travel around the world.

    B. Enter a marathon to stay as physically active as you can.

    C. Take as many risks as possible by going to dangerous places.

    D. Don't let a disability limit what you want to accomplish in life.

Real People, Events, and Information
Lesson 8 Summary

When answering questions about nonfiction, informational text, and biographies, remember the following tips:

- Authors organize nonfiction materials in many ways.
- Many nonfiction books and articles are written to give information.
- Know what kinds of learning resources are available to you.
- Decide which type of resource connects to your topic.
- Some informational materials, such as directions or instructions, are written to help you accomplish a task or do a job.
- Biographies and autobiographies tell true stories about people's lives.

Practice Passage

Directions: Read the passage, then answer the questions that follow.

Water from the Sun
by Angie Roney

Seventy-one percent of the earth's surface is covered with water. Yet only a very small percentage of this water is actually safe to drink. Most of the earth's water is salty. Although many sea creatures like this just fine, humans who drink only salt water will eventually die. Crops will also die if they are watered with salt water. Industry cannot use salt water in most situations, either. Salt water causes machinery to rust more quickly.

For thousands of years people have used the power of the sun to turn salt water into fresh water. Many people believe this is the answer to our growing need for water. The sun naturally draws water upward into the atmosphere in the form of water vapor. As the water vapor rises, the salt is left behind. The water vapor later returns to the earth in the form of fresh water (rain, sleet, and snow).

The process of separating salt and other minerals from water is called **distillation**. This process can be copied by humans. Many countries have large distillation plants that provide water to whole cities. You, too, can turn salt water into fresh water. The process is fun and easy, once you have the right materials together. Read the following directions to find out how to distill salt water into fresh water.

WHAT YOU WILL NEED:

1 large bowl

1 quart of seawater (If none is available, add 2 tablespoons of table salt to 1 quart of fresh water.)

1 medium-sized glass or jar

plastic wrap

1 large rubber band or long piece of string

2 small stones or other small, slightly heavy objects

lots of sunshine

INSTRUCTIONS:

Step 1: Pour the seawater or salt water into the large bowl.

Step 2: Place the glass or jar upright in the center of the bowl. The rim of the glass should be above the water level but below the top of the bowl. You may need to place a stone or other heavy object in the bottom of the glass to steady it. (Make sure the object is very clean.)

 **Step 3:** Use the plastic wrap to completely cover the top of the bowl. Do not pull the plastic wrap too tight.

Step 4: Use a large rubber band or string to fasten the wrap to the edge of the bowl.

Step 5: Place a small stone or other object on top of the wrap, centered over the glass or jar. The stone should be heavy enough to cause the wrap to sag at a point directly over the glass.

Step 6: Place the bowl in direct sunlight. (It should be a very warm day, preferably in summertime.) The heat of the sun will cause some of the water to turn into vapor and rise to the top. It will collect on the underside of the plastic wrap in the form of little <u>droplets</u>. The slant of the plastic caused by the stone will make the drops roll downward and drip into the glass.

Step 7: Once you have collected a bit of water in the glass, taste it. It might taste slightly <u>brackish</u> (salty), but it is safe to drink.

Sample Information Questions

1. How does the author compare humans to sea creatures?

   A. Drinking salt water is safe for sea creatures but not for humans.

   B. Both sea creatures and humans lack enough fresh water.

   C. Sea creatures can gain fresh water from rain; humans cannot.

   D. Neither sea creatures nor humans can drink "brackish" water.

2. What is the most likely reason the author wants you to taste the result of this experiment?

   A. so you don't waste natural resources

   B. so you can tell someone else about the experiment

   C. so you can tell that the experiment worked

   D. so you will not get thirsty while experimenting

3. If you wanted additional information on the process of separating salt from water, which of the following would be the best source?

   A. an online article about sea creatures

   B. a book titled *Experiments Using Rocks*

   C. a magazine article about distillation plants

   D. a newspaper story about pollution in big cities

4. What is the next step after you cover the top of the bowl with plastic wrap?

   A. Place a small stone on top of the wrap.

   B. Place the large bowl in direct sunlight.

   C. Place a glass or jar upright in the bowl's center.

   D. Fasten the wrap with string or a rubber band.

5. Why must you place the bowl in direct sunlight on a warm day?

   A. so the sun can draw vapor from the salt water

   B. so you can easily see the results of the experiment

   C. so the plastic wrap will stick to the bowl more tightly

   D. so the results of the experiment are known before dark

6. What is the author's main purpose for writing this passage?

   A. to entertain with a story about sea creatures

   B. to explain saltwater distillation using an experiment

   C. to tell how salt water causes machinery to rust

   D. to inform people about distillation plants in large cities

7. How is this passage organized? Do you think the organization is good for the passage? Explain your answer.

   _____

   _____

   _____

   _____

   _____

   _____

   _____

   _____

   _____

Additional Practice Questions

8. Which of the following sentences best summarizes the main idea of the passage?

   A. Fresh water is easier to make than salt water.

   B. The world needs more fresh water for drinking.

   C. Salt water can be changed to fresh water through distillation.

   D. Industry should discover ways to use salt water to run machinery.

9. Which of the following sentences from the passage is an opinion?

   A. Crops will also die if they are watered with salt water.

   B. The process is fun and easy, once you have the right materials together.

   C. The sun naturally draws water upward into the atmosphere in the form of water vapor.

   D. The heat of the sun will cause some of the water to turn into vapor . . .

10. What is the meaning of the word "droplets" as used in Step 6?

   A. lumps

   B. bubbles

   C. large pools

   D. small drops

11. Which of the following might be a good use for sea water?

   A. filling aquariums at a zoo

   B. watering crops on a farm

   C. cooling machinery at a factory

   D. washing engines at a garage

12. What would most likely happen if you forgot to place a small stone or object on top of the plastic wrap?

   A. The seawater will not heat up.

   B. The fresh water will not drip as easily into the glass.

   C. The seawater will not turn into vapor.

   D. The fresh water that is collected will taste salty.

13. Why do you think it might be important for people to know how to distill
    water? Use the passage to explain your answer.

    _____

    _____

    _____

    _____

    _____

    _____

    _____

    _____

    _____

    _____

14. What best describes the meaning of *brackish* as it is used in Step 7?
    A. strange color
    B. odd odor
    C. unsafe liquid
    D. salty flavor

Beyond the Basics

In this unit, you'll learn to polish the reading skills that you have been working on in Units 1 and 2. In order to truly understand what you are reading, it's important to go beyond the written words and read between the lines. This unit will help you do just that. Before you know it, you'll be making connections that will improve your understanding.

You'll also learn about the writer behind the writing, and find out what the author wants to accomplish in a story or nonfiction piece.

After studying this unit, you'll be better prepared to do well on any reading test.

In This Unit
- ◆ *Critical Reading Skills*
- ◆ *Getting to Know the Author*

Lesson 9

Critical Reading Skills

There are some things you just need to know, like your locker combination or when to keep your voice down to a whisper. These critical skills make your life at school easier.

In this lesson, you will learn some critical skills that will help make reading easier. You'll practice such reading techniques as making comparisons and contrasts, finding causes and effects, putting events in order, and connecting details to make inferences and predictions.

Alike and Different

Read the following passage. Look for words and phrases that show how the characters are alike and different.

> The first morning in her new house, Ellie looked out the window and saw a boy about her age walking to school. He was tall and thin, and the way he walked reminded her of a camel. He took long, slow steps, and his whole body seemed to float up and down, as if carried by gentle waves of water. His shirt was buttoned crookedly, his hair went every which way, and his socks were two different colors.
>
> Ellie finished putting her lunch and notebooks in her school bag. When she looked up again, she thought she was seeing things. There was the same boy passing her house again. This time, however, his hair was neater. But he had exactly the same walk, the same clothes, and the same mismatched socks.
>
> She pressed her face to the window and looked up the street. No, there were two boys—identical twins.
>
> When Ellie got to school, she learned that these boys were the locally famous Humphrey twins, Hector and Horace. They *never* walked together because they didn't much like each other. That seemed funny to Ellie, since they both looked and acted exactly the same.

Authors often compare and contrast things in their writing. Noticing when they do this—and knowing how to compare and contrast things yourself—will help you better understand the things you read. Here are a few tips to help you practice this skill.

Tip 1 **Look for words that show comparisons or contrasts.**

Reading passages are often loaded with words that show how things are alike and different. We call this **comparing and contrasting**. The following list shows just a few compare/contrast words you should look for.

Alike	Different
both	but
like	unlike
all	however
too	instead of
just as	different from
similar to	not the same as
the same as	on the other hand

Some words that describe can be turned into compare/contrast words by adding a prefix or suffix. For example, *fast* can be turned into the compare/contrast word *faster* by adding *er*. Here are a few more examples.

Words Using . . .	Examples		
-er	bigg**er**	short**er**	loud**er**
-est	tall**est**	smart**est**	creepi**est**
more and most	**more** curious	**most** handsome	
less and least	**less** colorful	**least** frightened	

1. Now go back to the passage about the Humphrey twins. Look at the passage and underline any compare or contrast words you see.

2. The twins are alike because they both
   A. have mismatched socks.
   B. have the same neat hair.
   C. have matching notebooks.
   D. enjoy each other's company.

3. How are the twins different from one another?
   A. One of them is tall and thin; the other is short and muscular.
   B. One of them walks like a camel; the other walks like a giraffe.
   C. One of them has messy hair; the other has hair that is neater.
   D. One of them wears matching socks; the other wears mismatched socks.

Tip 2 **Compare details.**

What if you search for compare-and-contrast words but don't find any? You can still figure out similarities and differences. You just have to put your detective skills to work.

Read the following fable. It describes two birds. Pay attention to the details the author gives about each character.

The Peacock and the Crane

adapted from a fable by Aesop

One day a peacock came upon a crane. The peacock began making fun of the crane and criticized the color of his plain feathers.

"I am dressed in bright gold and purple feathers," said the peacock. "I am a dazzling sight to see. You wear only drab white feathers."

"But with these feathers," replied the crane, "I can fly to the highest mountain and sing near the stars. You can only hop along near the ground." ❖

4. In the following boxes, list as many details as you can about the two birds.

Peacock	Crane

5. How are the birds different?
   A. The crane can fly, but the peacock cannot.
   B. The peacock can fly, but the crane cannot.
   C. The crane brags about his beauty, but the peacock is humble.
   D. The peacock has plain feathers, but the crane has colorful feathers.

Read the passage. It will help you understand the information and questions that follow.

First One Thing, Then Another
by Malia Hewson

I was reading a book in my room, quietly minding my own business, when Mom walked in carrying her only pair of tennis shoes. Her hair was pulled back in a ponytail and she was dressed in shorts and a T-shirt, ready to go for her nightly run. I could tell by the way her lips were pressed tightly together that she wasn't too happy.

"Malia," she said, holding up her left tennis shoe, "what happened to my shoelace?"

I knew she wasn't going to like it, so I set down my book and took a deep breath. "If you really want to know, it's Frally's fault. She's the one who wanted to play baseball this afternoon."

"And what does *that* have to do with my shoelace?" she said, first giving me a puzzled look, and then staring at her laceless shoe.

"Well," I began, "during the last inning of the game, I hit the ball just past second base, where I happened to park my bike."

"And?"

"And because my bike got in the way of the ball, my back reflector broke. It just plain cracked—

"I've got quite a swing," I added, smiling.

"Keep going," Mom said.

"Anyway," I went on, "I know you don't like me riding around without a reflector—it not being safe and all—so I stopped at the bike store on my way home from the game and bought a new one."

"What does that have to do with my shoelace?"

"I'm getting to that. After I got home and took off the broken reflector, I went inside to fix a snack. Except when I came back out, I couldn't find the screw I was supposed to use to attach the new reflector. I looked through the toolbox to see if I could find another one that was the right size, but I didn't have any luck. So I got to thinking, and I remembered that when Dad and I put the latch on the gate in the backyard, we used a screw just about the size I needed. Well, I took off the latch, and the screw fit perfectly. The only thing is, the gate wouldn't shut then; and, of course, I didn't want Skippy to get out of the backyard, so that's where your shoelace comes in. I used it to tie the gate shut."

"Why didn't you use one of your own shoelaces?"

"Well, I was wearing my shoes, and yours were just sitting by the front door."

"What if I'd been out running?"

"Then I'd have to do some explaining to Dad tonight."

"Where *are* his running shoes?" Mom asked. I could see she was getting an idea. ❖

Life is full of thorny little problems. Problems usually have some sort of reason, or cause, behind them.

Recognizing problems, causes, effects, and solutions in reading passages will help you better understand the things you read.

Tip 3 **Identify the order of events in the passage.**

One way to spot problems and their causes is to list events in the order they occurred. By putting events in order, you can more easily see how one event leads to the next. Fill in the following timeline with the letter of each event listed below, then use it to answer the questions that follow.

    A. Malia loses the screw to the new reflector.

    B. Malia uses her mom's shoelace to tie the gate shut.

    C. Malia's friend asks her to play baseball.

    D. Malia takes the latch off the gate.

    E. Malia breaks the reflector on her bike.

    F. Malia's mom is upset because her shoelace is missing.

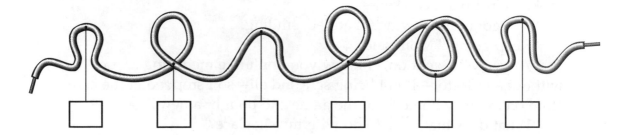

6. Why does Malia take the latch off the gate?

    A. The latch is broken.

    B. Her mom wants to go running.

    C. She needs a screw to attach the reflector.

    D. She doesn't want Skippy to get out of the backyard.

7. What is Malia's mother most likely thinking about doing at the end of the story?

    A. asking Frally if she wants to play baseball

    B. having Malia put the latch back on the gate

    C. going for a run in another pair of tennis shoes

    D. taking a shoelace from one of Dad's running shoes

Tip 4 **Sometimes writers give you clues to help you predict what is going to happen later in the story.**

These clues are called **foreshadowing**. Foreshadowing can help you predict what is going to happen later in the passage. A foreshadowing clue might read something like this:

> Approaching the empty house with curiosity and confidence, the two boys had no idea of the danger that awaited them inside its crumbling walls.

Tip 5 **Look for the cause and effect of a problem.**

TEACHER: Jackie, you've been late to school every day since school began. What's the reason?

JACKIE: I can't help it. The sign on the street says, "School, go slow."

—from *101 School Jokes* by Sam Schultz

The reason behind a problem is its cause. What happens because of the problem is the effect.

the cause → *the problem* → *the effect*

One way to find the cause and effect of a problem is to look for special words in the passage.

Cause Words	Effect Words
cause	therefore
due to	led to / lead to
a result of	resulted in
because	as a result
on account of	so

As you read the following passage, underline any "cause" or "effect" words or phrases you see. Then answer the questions that follow.

Our seas and oceans are threatened by two dangers: pollution and overfishing. Oil spills cause the deaths of countless sea creatures and birds. They also ruin our beaches. Factories, farms, and towns dump sewage and dangerous chemicals into our waters, poisoning fish and shellfish. Eating these animals can lead to sickness and even death.

Overfishing reduces the fish population further, and some species do not reproduce fast enough to replace those that are caught. As a result, the number of cod, herring, and anchovies in some areas is dangerously low. And it isn't just fish that are threatened. Many species of whales have been hunted to the point that they, too, are now endangered.

8. According to the passage, what are some causes of pollution in our seas and oceans? Write your answer on the following lines.

_____

_____

_____

_____

_____

9. Which of the following problems is not given as a result of oil spills?
   A. deaths of birds   C. deaths of sea creatures
   B. polluted beaches   D. too little oil for factories

10. According to the passage, what are some of the results of overfishing? Write your answer on the following lines.

_____

_____

_____

_____

_____

11. According to the passage, one result of overfishing is that
    A. restaurants are closing in coastal towns.
    B. some types of fish are decreasing in number.
    C. people are poisoned by eating the remaining fish.
    D. beaches are littered with fish that have been poisoned.

Tip 6 **Put the problem and its cause into a "because" sentence.**

If you can't find any "cause" words, look for the cause of the problem on your own. Then link the problem and its cause in a "because" sentence. The following is an example.

Sarah's face went pale. A frog was in her milk.

Sarah's face went pale **because** a frog was in her milk.

Read the following paragraph, then answer Number 12.

Horsecars were the ancestors of electric streetcars. Like streetcars, horsecars ran on rails that had been laid in the streets. Instead of being moved along the rails by electricity, the cars were pulled by horses. The first horsecars were used in New York City in 1852. They soon came to be used in other cities across the country. Many people objected to the horsecars. Some people thought the horses were overworked or mistreated. And in some cities, the horses were unable to climb the steep hills where the rails were laid.

12. Why did some people object to the use of horsecars?

Some people objected to the use of horsecars **because**

_____

_____.

Now use your "because" sentence to answer Number 13.

13. One reason people objected to the use of horsecars is because they thought
    A. people should be willing to walk more.
    B. electricity was a better source of power.
    C. the horses weren't being treated properly.
    D. horsecars should be used only in large cities.

Tip 7 Use your knowledge of cause and effect and order of events to make inferences.

Guesses based on known facts are called **inferences**. You make inferences all the time in real life. You also make them when you read. By making inferences based on details, you form a conclusion about what you've read.

When authors write stories, they don't always fill in every detail. They let you figure out what is happening. Stories are more interesting that way. Besides, you're getting older. Authors understand that you don't need every little thing spelled out for you anymore.

When answering an inference or conclusion question, start with what you know. Then put the details together to make connections. The following tips will give you suggestions about what to do next.

Tip 8 Look for evidence in the passage to support your inferences and predictions.

Always try to base your answers on supporting evidence from the passage. Read the following paragraph to practice this tip.

> It was a cool, crisp morning. Kim slipped her book bag over her shoulders, hopped on her bike, and headed down Maple Street. Her tires made soft crunching sounds as she rolled through piles of dry leaves.

14. What time of year do you think it is? _____

15. How do you know? _____

16. Where do you predict Kim is going? _____

17. What clue tells you where Kim might be going?

_____

Tip 9 **Make sure that your inferences are based on facts.**

Good inferences aren't wild guesses. The more supporting evidence you have, the stronger your inferences and conclusions will be.

Read the following paragraph, then answer Number 18.

The mockingbird has one of the prettiest songs of any bird native to North America. That is probably why some states have adopted it as their state bird. The song of the mockingbird is actually a mix of the calls of many other birds. Each song is repeated two or three times before the bird starts another song. A mockingbird may know as many as 25 or 30 different birdsongs.

18. One inference you could make based on this paragraph is that the mockingbird
    A. is a fierce protector of its nest.
    B. is a much smarter bird than the pigeon.
    C. is loved by every citizen of North America.
    D. is named for its ability to imitate other birds.

Read each choice carefully. Underline any supporting evidence in the passage. Look at choice A. There is nothing in the passage about the mockingbird behaving as a fierce protector of its nest.

Look at choice B. Is there anything in the passage that says the mockingbird is smarter than the pigeon? No. Even if choice B were true, you cannot make such an inference from this passage.

Look at choice C. Does the passage actually say that every citizen of North America loves the mockingbird? No.

Now look at choice D. Does the passage talk about the mockingbird in terms of its ability to imitate the songs of other birds? Yes. Even if you didn't know that *mocking* means *imitating*, you could probably infer that choice D is the best answer.

Critical Reading Skills
Lesson 9 Summary

When answering critical reading skills questions, remember the following tips:

- Look for words that show comparisons or contrasts.
- Compare details.
- Identify the order of events in the passage.
- Sometimes writers give you clues to help you predict what is going to happen later in the story.
- Look for the cause and effect of a problem.
- Put the problem and its cause into a "because" sentence.
- Use your knowledge of cause and effect and order of events to make inferences.
- Look for evidence in the passage to support your inferences and predictions.
- Make sure that your inferences are based on facts.

Practice Passage

Directions: Read the passage and answer the questions that follow.

Clouds
by Ted Remington

1   Almost every day, you see clouds in the sky. When it's raining, they cover the sky. Even when it's sunny, a few wispy clouds are usually floating around. Maybe you've seen big puffy clouds shaped in ways that remind you of animals or people. But have you noticed how many different kinds of clouds there are?

2   Even though we see clouds all the time, lots of people don't know that different kinds of clouds have their own names, are made out of different things, and float around different parts of the sky. Scientists have come up with names for almost every sort of cloud, but there are four main categories.

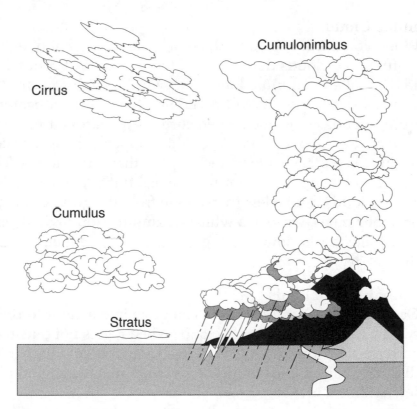

Cirrus Clouds

3   **Cirrus** clouds are the thin, white, delicate little clouds that sort of look like feathers in the sky. You often see these clouds on sunny days. Cirrus clouds are the highest of all clouds, floating four or five miles above the earth. Sometimes cirrus clouds don't seem to move across the sky very quickly because they are so far away. But actually, they can travel across

the sky at 200 miles an hour. Because the temperature several miles up is below freezing, cirrus clouds are made of ice crystals instead of water drops (as most other clouds are). Since cirrus clouds are made almost completely of ice, they do not cause rain. The ice crystals are too light to drop down. If you see cirrus clouds in the sky, you won't need your umbrella.

Stratus Clouds

4   On other days, you may look out your window and see the sky covered with a cloud like a blanket. When the sky is overcast and gray, the cloud you're looking at is called **stratus**. These clouds look like a smooth, even sheet. Stratus clouds are much closer to the ground than cirrus clouds. They can be up to one mile above the earth's surface, but they can also be much lower. When a stratus cloud comes all the way down to the ground, we get fog. Stratus clouds are made of tiny water drops. Because the drops are so small, they often do not fall to the ground. Sometimes, however, stratus clouds can produce light rain or snow (but not usually big storms).

Cumulus Clouds

5   When you think of clouds, the first kind you probably think of are the big puffy white clouds that look as if they're made of cotton balls. These clouds are called **cumulus** clouds. The word cumulus means "heap" or "pile," which is a good way of describing their fluffy appearance. Cumulus clouds are formed when currents of warm air make their way into the cold air above them. When this happens, the water vapor in the air begins to condense into water droplets that form clouds. The warm air continues to pile up the vapor into the big, fluffy, white clouds we see. Cumulus clouds can be less than a mile from the ground but can go as high as four miles. Once in a while, a cumulus cloud will drop a bit of rain. Just like cirrus clouds, though, we usually see them when the weather is dry.

Cumulonimbus Clouds

6   Occasionally, a cumulus cloud can grow into a **cumulonimbus** cloud. This is the fourth main type of cloud. When it gets hot outside, the warm air currents keep pushing the water vapor higher and higher. Instead of small fluffy white clouds, huge dark clouds are created and piled up, somewhat like a tower.

7   Cumulonimbus clouds usually start near the ground and pile up several miles high. They are sometimes called "thunderheads" because they create thunderstorms with lots of rain and, sometimes, hail. If you see a cumulonimbus cloud, be ready to get inside quickly. These clouds almost always create thunder, lightning, rain, and dangerous winds. Cumulonimbus clouds can be some of the most <u>imposing</u> clouds you'll ever see, so make sure you watch them from a safe, dry place! ❖

Sample Critical Reading Skills Questions

1. What do cirrus and cumulus clouds have in common?

    A. Both move very quickly.

    B. Neither is likely to produce rain.

    C. Both look like piles of cotton balls.

    D. Both are made mainly of ice crystals.

2. Which of the following is one way in which stratus clouds differ from cumulus clouds?

    A. Stratus clouds are white.

    B. Stratus clouds are big and fluffy.

    C. Stratus clouds can produce fog.

    D. Stratus clouds look like feathers in the sky.

3. Write details from the passage to show how cirrus and cumulonimbus clouds are alike or different.

Cirrus Clouds	Cumulonimbus Clouds

4. What is one result of the long distance between the earth and cirrus clouds?

    A. Cirrus clouds appear to move very slowly.

    B. Cirrus clouds appear to move very quickly.

    C. Cirrus clouds look like dark feathers in the sky.

    D. Cirrus clouds look as if they're made of cotton balls.

5. Why are cumulonimbus clouds also called "thunderheads"?

    A. They create cumulus clouds that bring thunderstorms.

    B. They usually bring thunder, lightning, and rain.

    C. The tops of the clouds are shaped like thunderbolts.

    D. They are usually dark gray and look dangerous.

6. Based on this passage, you could conclude that the prefix *strato* means
    A. pile or heap.
    B. dark or heavy.
    C. curly or wispy.
    D. sheetlike or layered.

7. When you see cirrus clouds in the sky, you can predict the weather will probably be
    A. clear.
    B. foggy.
    C. snowy.
    D. stormy.

8. What causes cumulonimbus clouds to be so dangerous?
    A. They are low to the ground.
    B. They are filled with water vapor.
    C. They create lightning and high winds.
    D. They are dark and piled up like a tower.

9. Fill in the diagram with a description of the three other types of clouds.

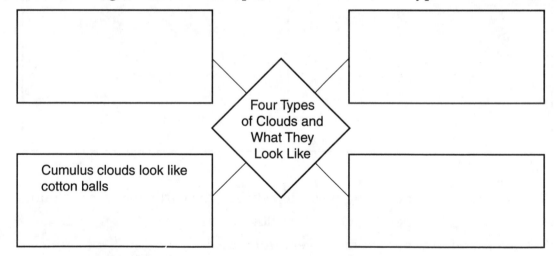

Additional Practice Questions

10. Which sentence best summarizes the main idea of this passage?

    A. Clouds can be dangerous.

    B. Clouds are made of water drops.

    C. There are many different kinds of clouds.

    D. Some clouds can be shaped like animals.

11. If you wanted to find out more about clouds and how they are made, which of the following books would be most helpful?

    A. *Clouds and the Weather*

    B. *101 Science Experiments for Students*

    C. *Hurricanes, Tornadoes, and Blizzards*

    D. *Conquering the Clouds: The Invention of the Airplane*

12. In paragraph 7, it says that cumulonimbus clouds can be some of the most imposing clouds you'll ever see. What does the word *imposing* mean?

    A. innocent

    B. disgusting

    C. impressive

    D. permanent

13. Which of the following statements from the passage is an opinion?

    A. Because the temperature several miles up is below freezing, cirrus clouds are made of ice crystals . . .

    B. When the sky is overcast and gray, the cloud you're looking at is called stratus.

    C. Cumulus clouds are formed when currents of warm air make their way into the cold air above them.

    D. Cumulonimbus clouds can be some of the most imposing clouds you'll ever see, so make sure you watch them from a safe, dry place!

Lesson 10

Getting to Know the Author

Imagine that you walk back to your desk from a trip to the pencil sharpener and find this note.

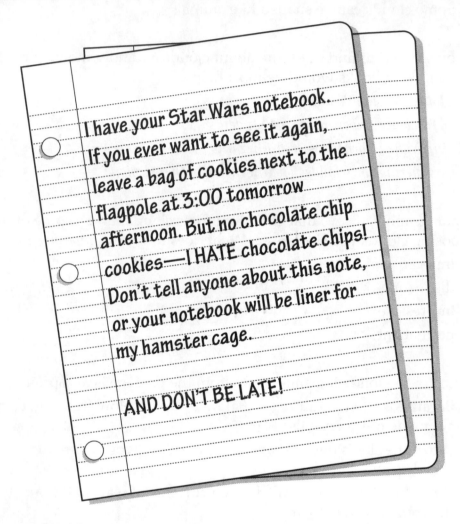

I have your Star Wars notebook. If you ever want to see it again, leave a bag of cookies next to the flagpole at 3:00 tomorrow afternoon. But no chocolate chip cookies—I HATE chocolate chips! Don't tell anyone about this note, or your notebook will be liner for my hamster cage.

AND DON'T BE LATE!

You rack your brain trying to figure out who the thief is. Who would take your *Star Wars* notebook, the one with the awesome picture on the front? Who hates chocolate chips? Who has a hamster? And that last line sounds rather threatening. Do you know *anyone* with such a nasty attitude?

The Writer Behind the Writing

You can tell a lot about a writer from the things he or she has written. By reading closely, you can learn an author's purpose and point of view. The following tips will give you practice in reading closely and getting to know the authors and some of their techniques.

Tip 1 **Pay attention to the author's attitude and word choice.**

Have you ever been told that you have a good attitude, such as when you did something nice for your little brother, even though he was being a real pest? Or maybe there have been times when your attitude wasn't so good, such as the time you were not allowed to do something you really wanted to do, and you pouted for a whole day.

A person's **attitude** is how he or she generally feels about something. We each have different attitudes about different things. Authors have attitudes, too. The words they use are clues to those attitudes.

- A **positive** attitude supports an issue or problem. It might show happiness, hope, joy, excitement, pride, or any number of other "good" feelings.

- A **negative** attitude opposes an issue or problem. It might show sorrow, shame, fear, anger, or other "bad" feelings.

- A **neutral** attitude generally presents both sides of an issue or problem without taking sides. It doesn't show strong feelings one way or the other.

1. In the space provided after each paragraph, tell whether each author's word choice and attitude are *positive*, *negative*, or *neutral.*

Spinach is one of the world's greatest vegetables. It can be eaten fresh, in a lovely salad, steamed, or creamed in a casserole. I think everyone should enjoy at least one serving of spinach every day.

_____

Spinach is probably the most disgusting food I have ever eaten. It doesn't look or smell good—and it doesn't taste good, either. Spinach should be saved for Popeye and for hungry rabbits. I'd rather eat broccoli!

_____

Spinach is a leafy vegetable. People eat it raw or cooked. It is related to Swiss chard and beets. Originally, spinach came from southwest Asia. Persians used it for medicine. The English began growing it in the 1500s. Spinach is a source of vitamin C.

_____

Tip 2 **Determine the author's purpose for writing.**

Authors write for many reasons. As you read a passage, ask yourself, *Why did the author write this? What does he or she want to tell me? What does he or she want my reaction to be?*

Writing to inform

As you learned in Lesson 8, authors sometimes want to give you information. They might tell facts they think you will find interesting. They might explain or show how something works. They might give helpful hints, such as how to eat healthily or how to shop for a new bike.

The main purpose of passages like these is to **teach** or **inform**. Such passages usually give facts with little or no opinion. If there are two or more sides to an issue, the author generally presents all sides as having equal value.

Writing to explain

Another way authors can give information is to explain something. In this type of writing, the author might describe a new computer system, explain how it works, or give instructions on how to use it.

Writing to entertain

Sometimes authors just want to entertain you. They might try to amuse you with a humorous story, play, or poem. They might even try to frighten you with a scary tale. Other types of writing meant for entertainment include fantasy, mystery, adventure, science fiction—anything that you read "just for fun."

Writing to persuade

Sometimes authors want you to agree with them. They might criticize something they don't like. They might present a new idea for solving a problem and then argue for their idea. These authors often give plenty of facts to support their ideas. They may also compare their idea with an opposing idea.

These types of passages are usually filled with opinions. If there are two or more sides to an issue, the writer presents one side as being the best. The author is mainly trying to convince you to come over to his or her way of thinking. He or she might also want you to take some action based on what you've read. Advertising is a common form of persuasive writing. So are editorials, essays, and letters to the editor.

2. Draw a line from each type of publication to its most likely purpose.

newspaper editorial   to inform

guidebook with maps   to persuade

short story   to entertain

front-page news story   to explain

Read the following letter and answer the questions that follow.

Letter to the Editor

Dear Editor,

I read your article in last Sunday's *Gazette* titled "Pennies: Are They Worth It?" I, too, believe that we should do away with pennies. Many people do not like to carry pennies because they weigh down pockets or purses. Many families have jars full of pennies sitting around. They are worth so little that most people will not stoop to pick one up. The U.S. Mint has to keep making pennies because so many people do not spend them.

It is true that if we eliminated the penny, our money system would need to change. Merchants would have to set prices differently, or prices would need to be rounded to the nearest nickel. But we would not be the only country to try this. Other countries have also changed their money systems. The British have eliminated their farthing, which was much like our penny. And our own country has made similar changes in the past. In the 1800s, our government issued half-cent, two-cent, and three-cent coins.

As our lifestyles change and improve, our money system could stand some improvement, too.

Sincerely,

Albert Finestine

Albert Finestine

3. What is the author's purpose in this passage?
   A. to entertain with an interesting story
   B. to persuade others to support an idea
   C. to compare pennies with two-cent coins
   D. to explain the process of minting coins

4. How do you know the answer to Number 3?

   _____

   _____

   _____

Tip 3 Determine the author's viewpoint.

An author's **viewpoint** is his or her opinion about the topic. Figuring out the author's attitude and purpose will help you determine his or her viewpoint. Read the passage and answer the questions that follow.

> I'm getting sick of the Side Alley Guys. They're everywhere! First came their CDs and videos, then a movie, and now there's even Side Alley Guys' soda! I would understand all the hoopla if these six boys could sing, but they can't.
>
> If you agree with me, call your local radio and television stations. Tell them to stop feeding the Side Alley Guys craze and give more airtime to bands with real talent.

5. What is the author's attitude toward the musical group Side Alley Guys? (Circle one.)

          Positive   Negative   Neutral

6. What is the author's purpose for writing?
   A. to inform
   B. to describe
   C. to entertain
   D. to persuade

7. Which of these is the author's opinion?
    A. The Side Alley Guys' music is not very good.
    B. The Side Alley Guys' soda does not taste good.
    C. The Side Alley Guys' movie was not a success.
    D. The Side Alley Guys are more talented than most bands.

8. What is the author's point of view about the Side Alley Guys?
    A. They should sell more than one kind of soda.
    B. They should quit music to be in more movies.
    C. They should play instruments instead of sing.
    D. They should be given less attention by the media.

Tip 4 **Determine whether statements are *fact* or *opinion*.**

A **fact** statement can be checked out. Fact statements use words that have meanings everyone can agree on.

Examples of Fact Words		
square	round	broken
red	metal	forty
Egyptian	poison	striped
plastic	empty	closed

If your brother says, "You haven't cleaned your room in six weeks," he is making a statement of fact. His statement can be checked out. Other family members can be interviewed about when they last saw you clean your room.

An **opinion** statement cannot be checked out. Opinion statements use words that mean different things to different people.

Examples of Opinion Words		
beautiful	scary	exciting
ugly	funny	yucky
best	wonderful	boring
silly	awful	expensive

If your brother says, "Your room looks like a pigpen," he is making a statement of opinion. You might think your room looks more like a New York City street after a confetti parade. Your best friend, who is even messier than you, might think that your room looks super neat.

Next to each sentence, write an *F* for *fact* or an *O* for *opinion*.

_____ 9. Judy Blume writes interesting books.

_____ 10. The Ohio River is 981 miles long.

_____ 11. My neighbor is a great artist.

_____ 12. Lincoln Elementary School in Findlay, Ohio, has awesome school lunches.

_____ 13. Superman's secret identity is Kent Clark, a newspaper reporter for *The Daily Orbit*.

_____ 14. Kiko invited the entire class to her house for a party.

_____ 15. Roscoe Village is in Coshocton, Ohio.

Tip 5 **Notice whether the author supports opinions and suggestions with facts.**

Everyone has opinions, and most people like to share them. Unless you are reading a passage that is nothing more than a list of facts, you'll probably run into an author's opinions or suggestions in almost anything you read. But should you just accept whatever the author tells you? Not unless the author gives you good reasons to believe what the passage says. As a reader, you need to make sure the author supports what is said with facts.

Read the following part of a restaurant review.

> The House of Cabbage is the best restaurant ever! Everything I tried was awesome. I can't believe anyone would not love the food at The House of Cabbage. Trust me, you'll go crazy for the food at The House of Cabbage!

The author sure has a strong opinion about The House of Cabbage. There isn't much in the review to tell you why you should share this opinion, though. The author just says, "Trust me."

Now read another review of The House of Cabbage.

> The House of Cabbage is an excellent restaurant. The prices are reasonable. No dinner costs more than five dollars. The cooks are also very creative. They've come up with 83 different ways to serve cabbage! With so many choices, you'll probably have no problem finding one that you like. And whatever dinner you choose, you'll know that it will be good for you because cabbage is one of the healthiest foods you can eat.

This author also really likes the restaurant. In this review, however, the author gives several reasons that support this opinion.

16. Write three reasons the author gives that support the opinion that the House of Cabbage is an excellent restaurant.

_____

_____

_____

_____

Getting to Know the Author
Lesson 10 Summary

When answering questions about the author of a passage, remember the following tips:

- Pay attention to the author's attitude and word choice.
- Determine the author's purpose for writing.
- Determine the author's viewpoint.
- Determine whether statements are *fact* or *opinion*.
- Notice whether the author supports opinions and suggestions with facts.

Practice Passages

Directions: Read the passages, then answer the questions that follow each.

Passage 1:

from

Dismasted!

by Frank Robben

1   So now I know what it is like to be dismasted. Not fully, . . . but enough for the experience to be another notch in my list of little adventures in life. We were entering the Indian Ocean, west of Australia, going from one remote, but inhabited, small island to another; to be exact, from Christmas Island to the Cocos Keeling Islands, both owned and <u>administered</u> by Australia. A three to four day voyage, easy and short. We were having a wonderful sail, with fairly strong wind at right angles to the desired direction of the boat (a cruising sailor's favorite wind direction), and were making close to maximum speed using a large jib and full main sail. A little bit rough, with the boat slewing around some in the moderately rough seas, but nothing really uncomfortable. At 0200 I was in my bunk in the deckhouse, sort of awake, and Ali was at the helm, steering by hand to save the autopilot from unnecessary strain. There was a loud bang and then I heard the fluttering of sails and knew something

serious was wrong. Looking out, I could not really see anything, but the boom of the main sail was dragging in the water, and the boat was beginning to roll heavily in the waves. Ali said, "The mast is broken," and the fear of being dismasted leaped into reality.

2   . . . I could see that the top third of the mast had broken off and was dangling, upside down, from the remaining stump of the mast and dangling furiously from side to side. The sails were in the water and the deck on the starboard side was a tangle of wire and rope. The first thing to do was to get the lines and sails back aboard, tie things down, and then probably proceed under engine to our planned destination, Cocos Keeling. To do this without damaging the boat further, and especially without anyone getting hurt or falling overboard [was our main concern].

3   Miraculously the top part of the mainsail had come free from the broken upper third of the mast, still swinging 50 feet above deck from the remaining mast and threatening anyone underneath it. The mainsail did not appear to be badly damaged. Such was my [first measure] of the damage . . . With much tugging and pulling we then got the sail out of the water and put an extra line on the boom so it would not swing across the deck and hurt someone or break more gear.

4   Soon we had most of the broken equipment back on board, with a bit of sail and a few lines still trailing in the heaving ocean. It was still dark and windy, and I could not think of any way to secure the broken mast which was dangling [dangerously] high above deck and loudly banging against the mast and lower spreaders. Obviously it was slowly destroying everything it would reach, but I did not know what to do, and I knew I did not want to go up the mast, at night in the dark, trying to get a line on it to secure it . . . I then told everyone to go below and try and rest until daylight. I put Audrey on watch, to see if anything more disastrous might happen with the flaying[1] mast section, and climbed into my bunk and rested while listening to it beating against the shortened mast. ❖

[1] **flaying:** whipping or lashing

Sample Author Questions

1. Which of the following best describes what the author feels about the ocean?
   - A. disgust
   - B. anger
   - C. respect
   - D. boredom

2. Which of the following best describes the author's attitude about sailing?
   - A. positive
   - B. negative
   - C. neutral
   - D. very negative

3. What was the author's purpose for writing this passage?

   A. to persuade readers to learn the art of sailing

   B. to entertain readers with a true story of danger at sea

   C. to teach readers about emergency procedures on a sailing ship

   D. to describe the features of Christmas Island and the Cocos Keeling Islands

Passage 2:

A Dream Come True

by Jessica Renaud

1 On June 25, 1998, Karen Thorndike became the first woman from the United States to sail solo around the world. Aboard her 36-foot yacht, *Amelia*, Karen suffered many hardships before finishing her amazing high-seas journey. She returned safely to Hilo, Hawaii, 625 days after she left.

2 In a way, the trip had begun many years earlier when Karen first learned to sail. By the time she was a young woman, she had developed a lifelong love of the sea. During her many sailing trips, Karen dreamed about sailing around the world—alone. Finally, her dream came true.

3 Karen's first solo attempt, in 1995, ended quickly when *Amelia* needed major repairs. But, in 1996, Karen set off alone once more and successfully sailed more than 30,000 nautical miles.[1]

4 It was very important to Karen that she be able to share her remarkable journey with others. Luckily, technology and communication satellites helped her find a way to do just that. By contacting Karen's website on the Internet, friends and supporters from all over the world became an interactive part of her seafaring adventures. She sent location reports, weather updates, and reflections on her experiences. Karen knew that at any time of the day or night, someone might log on and become part of her difficult and dangerous <u>trek</u> around the world.

5 Karen has proven her ability to make dreams come true. But she doesn't plan to quit now. Thanks to technology, the rest of the world can watch as the adventures of Karen and *Amelia* continue. ❖

[1] **nautical mile:** a unit of distance used for navigating at sea or in the air; about 6,076 feet

Sample Author Questions

4. What is the author's main purpose for writing "A Dream Come True"?
   A. to persuade readers to sail the world alone
   B. to complain about the Internet connections
   C. to inform readers about Karen's adventures
   D. to entertain the reader with a made-up story

5. Which of the following sentences best describes the author's feelings toward Karen?
   A. Karen is to be congratulated on a great accomplishment.
   B. Karen's ship *Amelia* isn't very safe since it needed repairs.
   C. Karen has few supporters for her dangerous travels alone.
   D. Karen's interest in technology and communication is limited.

6. Which of the following best describes the author's attitude in "A Dream Come True"?
   A. negative because Karen was just lucky
   B. positive because Karen achieved a difficult goal
   C. negative because sailing is an uninteresting sport
   D. positive because Karen's story will encourage more people to sail

7. Which of the following sentences is an opinion?
   A. On June 25, 1998, Karen Thorndike became the first woman from the United States to sail solo around the world.
   B. Aboard her 36-foot yacht, *Amelia*, Karen suffered many hardships before finishing her amazing high-seas journey.
   C. She returned to Hilo, Hawaii, 625 days after she left.
   D. She sent location reports, weather updates, and reflections on her experiences.

Additional Practice Questions

8. In Passage 1, paragraph 1, the word *administered* means
   A. governed.
   B. applied to.
   C. performed on.
   D. acknowledged.

9. After reading "A Dream Come True," one could most likely predict that Karen will
   A. sail on *Amelia* once again.
   B. go to work on a cruise ship.
   C. become a computer specialist.
   D. be the first woman to visit another planet.

10. In paragraph 4 of "A Dream Come True," the author discusses Karen's "difficult and dangerous <u>trek</u> around the world." What is the meaning of the word *trek*?
    A. vacation
    B. journey
    C. accident
    D. settlement

11. Passage 1 and Passage 2 are similar because they both
    A. tell stories about losing a mast.
    B. tell about sailing the world alone.
    C. encourage readers to take up sailing.
    D. tell about the experiences people had at sea.

UNIT 4

Extending Your Reading Skills

Have you ever watched a TV news program about something you first learned from a newspaper or magazine? Information comes from all sorts of places, and it's important to draw conclusions about a topic by using a variety of sources. By learning about the topic from different places, you'll get a better understanding of the information.

Throughout this workbook, you have practiced reading different types of passages and learned some new reading skills along the way. This unit will take you a step further by helping you make comparisons between similar informational topics discussed by two different sources. You'll also have a chance to extend your reading skills to information found in charts, tables, graphs, and maps.

In This Unit
◆ *Comparing Nonfiction Passages*
◆ *Reading Across Genres*
◆ *Information at a Glance*

Lesson 11

Comparing Nonfiction Passages

"Hey, Rodrigo, I just read a book about Christopher Columbus coming to the Americas with his three ships, the *Niña*, the *Pinta*, and the *Santa Maria*. It's really cool."

"Oh, yeah? I just read a book about the great Admiral Zheng He. This Chinese explorer was sailing across vast oceans years before Columbus tried it."

"I suppose their stories are pretty much the same, huh?"

"Well, both admirals sailed the seas, that's true. But that's where the likeness stops. On his first voyage, Zheng He traveled with a fleet of more than 300 ships and almost 30,000 sailors."

"Wow! Can I borrow your book about Zheng He?"

"Sure, if I can read your book about Columbus."

"It's a deal. When we're finished reading the books, we can compare the two admirals and their voyages."

"Great idea. See ya after school!"

The same story can be told in similar or different ways. And stories with similar topics can be told the same way or in different ways. This is because writers make choices about what to include, what to leave out, what to stress as important, and how to organize the story or information.

Read the following accounts of the same event. Look carefully to see how the two accounts are alike and different.

Passage 1

The first account of the event is from *The World Book Encyclopedia*, 2001.

In 1830, a famous race was held between a horse and a steam locomotive, the *Tom Thumb*. Peter Cooper, a New York manufacturer and builder of the locomotive, wanted to convince officials of the Baltimore and Ohio Railroad to use locomotives rather than

Peter Cooper's original *Tom Thumb* sits on tracks of the Baltimore and Ohio Railroad in this photo taken sometime between 1900 and 1950. The steam-powered locomotive was built in 1829.

horses to pull their trains. The horse won the race after an engine belt slipped on the *Tom Thumb*. But this defeat was only a minor setback for the locomotive, which was sometimes called the "iron horse."

Passage 2

The Great Race

adapted from the personal recollections of
John Hazlehurst Boneval Latrobe, published in 1868

On this date in 1830, the writer enjoyed a "most interesting" 13-mile journey in an open railroad car pulled by the first railroad steam engine, named Tom Thumb. *He goes on to describe a race between a gray horse "of great beauty and power" and the steam engine. Each pulled a railroad car on parallel tracks. This was to be a chance for the steam engine to prove to the world that it could travel as fast as a horse. Here is Mr. Latrobe's account.*

September 18, 1830
Baltimore and Ellicott's Mills, Maryland

The start being even, away went horse and engine, the snort of the one and the puff of the other keeping time and tune. At first, the gray had the best of it, for his effort could give him quick results, while the engine had to wait until the turning wheels set the blower to work.

The horse was perhaps a quarter of a mile ahead when the safety valve of the engine lifted and the thin blue vapor coming from it showed an excess of steam. The blower whistled. The steam blew off in vapory clouds, the pace increased, the passengers shouted, the engine gained on the horse. Soon it caught up with him—the race was neck and neck, nose and nose—then the engine passed the horse, and a great shout cheered the victory!

But the shout was not repeated, for just at this moment, when the gray's master was about giving up, the band that drove the pulley, which drove the blower, slipped off the drum. The safety valve ceased to scream, and the engine, for want of breath, began to wheeze and pant.

In vain, Mr. Cooper, who was his own engineman and fireman, attempted to replace the band upon the wheel. He tried to urge the fire with light wood. The horse gained on the machine and passed. And although the band was soon replaced, and steam again did its best, the horse was too far ahead to be overtaken and came in the winner of the race.

But the real victory was still with Mr. Cooper. He had held fast to his faith in the steam engine and had shown its usefulness beyond question. ❖

Tip 1 **Compare details within the passages.**

When you're asked to compare two passages, first see whether both give the same details. In this case, both passages tell about the horse and locomotive racing. But one passage gives many more details.

1. Find three important details that are given in both passages and underline them.

2. First, listen to your teacher's instructions. Then, with your classmates, discuss how the articles differ in organization and author's treatment of the topic.

Tip 2 **Compare the writers' attitudes and purposes.**

Is one passage more positive or negative than the other? Are both neutral? Keep in mind the writers' attitudes and purposes as you make comparisons.

3. Which of the following best describes Latrobe's attitude toward the steam engine?
   A. neutral
   B. positive
   C. negative
   D. uncertain

4. What is the main purpose of the encyclopedia excerpt?
   A. to persuade readers to ride trains
   B. to describe the operation of a steam engine
   C. to entertain readers with a funny story about a race
   D. to inform readers about a race between a horse and a steam locomotive

5. Which passage is more entertaining? Why?

_____

_____

_____

_____

_____

Tip 3 **Look for ways in which one passage adds to your understanding of another.**

Sometimes the information given in one passage will provide you with a deeper understanding of information contained in a second passage. Notice how Latrobe's passage carefully describes the details of the race against the horse. The encyclopedia excerpt tells that the locomotive is sometimes called an "iron horse."

6. How does Latrobe's description of the race add to your understanding of the term "iron horse"?

_____

_____

_____

_____

_____

_____

_____

_____

_____

Comparing Nonfiction Passages
Lesson 11 Summary

When comparing nonfiction passages, remember the following tips:

- Compare details within the passages.
- Compare the writers' attitudes and purposes.
- Look for ways in which one passage adds to your understanding of another.

Practice Passages

Directions: Read both passages, then answer the questions that follow.

Passage 1

From the *Long Pass Ledger*, Saturday, October 13, 2001

Willie Nelson Farm Aid benefit set for October 21

by Red Gomez
Ledger Staff Writer

Willie Nelson performs at Farm Aid 2001 on September 29.

Residents of Long Pass and the surrounding area will be traveling in large numbers to Austin on October 21, where they will participate in *Willie Nelson's 10K for Farm Aid*, a 10-kilometer race. The event is being produced by RunTex, a local runners' store.

The race will begin at 6 P.M. and will include a 5K Run for those unable to run the longer distance and a 5K Fun Walk for those who are unable to run. Following the race at 8 P.M., Austin's own Willie Nelson will treat the race <u>participants</u> to a music concert.

Willie Nelson and fellow musicians Neil Young and John Mellencamp founded Farm Aid in 1985. Since then, the organization has raised more than $16 million to help farmers and rural organizations. Nelson, who is president of Farm Aid, says, "The fight to save family farms isn't just about farmers. It's about making sure there is a safe and healthy food supply for all of us. It's about jobs, from Main Street to Wall Street. It's about a better America."

Local rancher Maurice Pringle says, "This is an opportunity for Long Pass to show support for a good cause, and be part of something that will, hopefully, become a tradition. This race is just another way Willie Nelson shows his loyalty to the people who helped make him. His life has been an inspiration. He was born in a farm town during the Great Depression, and through his talents, he has become an international star. So what does he do with his star power? He helps the people who helped get him started."

Pringle is a member of a local group called *Family Farmers First*. Members of that organization and other Long Pass residents will meet in the Community Center parking lot at noon on October 21 and then travel to Austin.

Nelson promises the participants a good time and says, "It's a pleasure to host this event. I invite everyone to come to Austin and enjoy a day of running and music in support of Farm Aid."

Passage 2

Jennifer Lee's diary entry, October 22, 2001:

Dear Diary,

Yesterday I went to Austin with my parents and my younger brother Justin to run in a 10-kilometer race. I had a really great time. Dad says the entry fee we paid will be used to help family farmers, which I think is a pretty neat thing to do. Dad and I ran the 10-kilometer course. Justin and Mom decided to walk the 5-kilometer course instead. Although 5K is a fairly short walk, you wouldn't know it from listening to Justin. He complained the whole day.

After the race, there was a super concert. The main attraction was country star Willie Nelson, who lives in Austin and who started Farm Aid, the organization that benefited from the race. I don't know much about Willie Nelson, except that he's really famous, plus he's kinda old. Dad says Willie's really just a kid at heart. "He thinks like a young person," Dad says. I don't know what Dad means when he says that, but when I get old, I hope I can think like a young person, too.

Anyway, Willie was just great! Everybody says they're going to have the run again next year. I can't wait.

Justin, on the other hand, says to count him out if they have the race next year. "Mom wouldn't let me play with my computer games," he said. "I was bored out of my mind, and there were too many people wandering around. Besides, who cares about Willie Nelson? He's old, his fans are old, and his guitar looks as if it has been run over by a truck."

Justin is such a creep—and so <u>immature</u>!

That's all for now.

Jennifer

Sample Comparison Questions

1. How is the purpose of each passage similar?
   A. Both persuade the reader to participate in the run.
   B. Both describe Willie Nelson's commitment to Farm Aid.
   C. Both inform the reader about specific family farm problems.
   D. Both explain how Willie Nelson became an international star.

2. What is one way these two passages are alike?
   A. Both are fiction.
   B. Both are newspaper articles.
   C. Both tell about Willie Nelson's 10-kilometer race.
   D. Both tell about the *Family Farmers First* organization.

3. What is one way the two passages are different?
   A. One is fiction; the other is nonfiction.
   B. One tells about Willie Nelson's concert; the other does not.
   C. One is meant to be read by many; the other by the writer alone.
   D. One talks about Willie Nelson's Farm Aid program; the other does not.

4. How does the author of Passage 1 organize his material?
   A. by discussing events in the order that those events happen
   B. by introducing a problem and then giving the solution to that problem
   C. by covering least important information to most important information
   D. by giving one point with its supporting details, then going to the next point with its supporting details, and so on

5. Based on the passages, both writers would agree that
   A. Willie Nelson is an excellent runner.
   B. Willie Nelson is one of the founders of Farm Aid.
   C. Willie Nelson is a kid at heart and thinks like a young person.
   D. Willie Nelson is a member of the Long Pass *Family Farmers First* group.

Additional Practice Questions

6. In the second paragraph of Passage 1, what does the word *participants* mean?
   A. people who win the race
   B. people who arrange the race
   C. people who take part in the race
   D. people who finish part of the race

7. According to Passage 1, Willie Nelson, Neil Young, and John Mellencamp founded Farm Aid in
   A. 1965.
   B. 1975.
   C. 1985.
   D. 1995.

8. Based on the newspaper article, who is a member of the *Family Farmers First* organization?
   A. Neil Young
   B. Willie Nelson
   C. Maurice Pringle
   D. John Mellencamp

9. In Passage 2, which person least enjoys the event?
   A. Jennifer
   B. Jennifer's dad
   C. Jennifer's mom
   D. Jennifer's brother

10. In the fifth paragraph of Passage 2, the word *immature* means
    A. not mature.
    B. mature early.
    C. partly mature.
    D. wrongly mature.

11. Why do you think Willie Nelson decided to help the farmers? Use details from the passages to help support your answer.

_____

_____

_____

_____

_____

_____

_____

_____

_____

_____

12. Using details from both passages, explain the purpose of the Farm Aid organization.

_____

_____

_____

_____

_____

Lesson 12

Reading Across Genres

Writers, like everybody else, have their own ideas and opinions regarding the people and things they write about. Because of this, writers can deal with the same subject and the same theme in many different ways. Even if they are writing about the same subject, each writer views the story somewhat differently, writes for different purposes and audiences, and may use different genres.

Comparing genres

In this part of the lesson, you will compare and answer questions about two paired passages, each in a different genre. Paired passages will always have some common location, characters, theme, or idea.

The two short passages that follow, are about different subjects, but they have a common connection. First, you'll read a nonfiction magazine advertisement for the state of Alaska, our northernmost state. Then you'll read a fictional passage that is set along the Alaskan border in Canada's Yukon Territory.

As you read each passage, think about what each one is mainly about and why it was written. Then you'll learn how to make comparisons across the two texts.

Passage 1:

First, read this advertisement for Alaska.

Come to Alaska

Many people think of Alaska as only snowy, icy wilderness—the land of igloos and sled-dog races. For the half-million people who live here and the countless others who visit each year, Alaska is much, much more.

Separated from the "lower 48" states by almost 500 miles of Canadian territory, Alaska is perfect for a real getaway. Visit our bustling cities and historic coastal towns, where you can enjoy our many museums, theaters, and restaurants. Numerous festivals are held across the state throughout the year. And don't pass up our smaller villages, such as Saxman, home of the world's largest collection of authentic totem poles.

Settlers came seeking their fortunes in furs in the 1700s, gold in the 1800s, and oil during the 1900s. We believe that future generations will come in search of Alaska's most abundant treasure—its landscape. Alaska is the largest state in the Union, more than twice the size of Texas. Much of it is still undisturbed by humans—rolling hills, sparkling lakes, majestic glaciers, swampy river valleys, and big-sky plains. Forests cover almost a third of the state. Alaska boasts the 16 highest mountain peaks in North America, along with several active volcanoes. Whether it is snowskiing, kayaking, fishing, or hiking, you'll find it all here.

Alaska's climate is as varied as its landscape. Warm winds that blow in from the ocean create a mild climate in the southern regions. During the summer, the sun shines about 20 hours a day. Average precipitation (rain, snow, and sleet) is about 55 inches per year. Average temperatures across the state range between –11° F in the winter to 59° F in the summer.

Come to Alaska. You'll find out why it is one of the fastest-growing states in the country. And maybe you'll decide to stay.

Passage 2:

Now read this fictional passage about the dangers of winter weather in the far north near the border of Alaska and the Yukon Territory.

This excerpt from Jack London's short story tells of a traveler caught in a bone-numbing world where it is 60 degrees below zero, and where a fire means the difference between life and death.

from

To Build a Fire

by Jack London

The old-timer on Sulphur Creek was right, . . . a man should travel with a partner. He beat his hands, but failed in exciting any sensation. Suddenly he bared both hands, removing the mittens with his teeth. He caught the whole bunch [of matches] between the heels of his hands. His arm muscles not being frozen enabled him to press the hand heels tightly against the matches. Then he scratched the bunch along his leg. It flared into flame, seventy sulphur matches at once! There was no wind to blow them out. He kept his head to one side to escape the strangling fumes, and held the blazing bunch to the birch bark. As he so held it, he became aware of sensation in his hand. His flesh was burning. He could smell it. Deep down below the surface he could feel it. The sensation developed into pain that grew acute.[1] And still he endured it, holding the flame of the matches clumsily to the bark that would not light readily because his own burning hands were in the way, absorbing most of the flame.

At last, when he could endure no more, he jerked his hands apart. The blazing matches fell sizzling into the snow, but the birch bark was alight. He began laying dry grasses and the tiniest twigs on the flame. He could not pick and choose, for he had to lift the fuel between the heels of his hands. Small pieces of rotten wood and green moss clung to the twigs, and he bit them off as well as he could with his teeth. He cherished the flame carefully and awkwardly. It meant life, and it must not perish. The withdrawal of blood from the surface of his body now made him begin to shiver, and he grew more awkward. A large piece of green moss fell squarely on the little fire. He tried to poke it out with his fingers, but his shivering frame made him poke too far, and he disrupted the nucleus of the little fire, the burning grasses and tiny twigs separating and scattering. He tried to poke them together again, but in spite of the tenseness of the effort, his shivering got away with him, and the twigs were hopelessly scattered. Each twig gushed a puff of smoke and went out. The fire provider had failed. ❖

[1] **acute:** severe

Tip 1 **Determine how the main ideas of the passages are alike or different.**

When you're asked to compare passages, first see how each passage deals with its main idea. In this case, the passages both tell about life in the far north. Remember, each passage is written from a different point of view, and for a different purpose.

1. Which of the following best describes one of the key ideas in both passages?
   A. Alaska is more than twice the size of Texas.
   B. It's not easy to light a fire when your fingers are frozen.
   C. It is very cold during the winter months in the far north.
   D. Alaska is filled with museums, theaters, and restaurants.

Tip 2 **Compare details in the two passages.**

To **compare** things is to show how they are alike and different. Think about how characters, settings, events, and ideas are alike or different.

2. When your teacher instructs you to do so, discuss with your classmates the theme of the passages and how the key ideas and details are alike and different.

3. What is the main idea in Passage 1?
   A. Alaska is a great state to choose for a vacation.
   B. Alaska is 500 miles away from the lower 48 states.
   C. Alaska has the world's largest collection of totem poles.
   D. In Alaska, the sun shines 20 hours a day during the summer.

4. What is the main idea in Passage 2?
   A. Lands as far north as Alaska and the Yukon are very dangerous in winter.
   B. In the far north, a man should travel with a partner and carry extra matches.
   C. It's difficult to build a decent fire out of small pieces of rotten wood and twigs.
   D. Withdrawal of blood from the body's surface can produce severe shivering.

Tip 3 **Compare the purposes of the two passages.**

Authors usually select a genre that they consider most suited to their purpose. An author probably wouldn't write a cookbook in poetry, for example. Review the two passages you have just read and answer Numbers 5 and 6.

5. What is the purpose of Passage 1?
   A. to persuade readers to visit Alaska
   B. to inform readers about the history of Alaska
   C. to describe Alaska's sparkling lakes and majestic glaciers
   D. to entertain readers with an interesting story about Alaska

6. What is the purpose of Passage 2?
   A. to persuade readers to travel with a partner
   B. to inform readers about the proper way to build a fire
   C. to describe the rugged terrain of Canada's Yukon Territory
   D. to entertain the reader with a fictional story of hardship and danger

Tip 4 **Use one passage to help you understand the other.**

As you learned in Lesson 11, sometimes one passage helps you understand another. Making connections between passages will also help you better understand each of them.

7. What do readers learn from "To Build a Fire" that will help them better understand "Come to Alaska"?
   A. Stay out of Alaska and the far north unless you absolutely have to go there.
   B. When visiting Alaska or the far north, be prepared to build lifesaving fires.
   C. Roads and trails throughout the far north are primitive and dangerous to travel.
   D. Think twice about winter vacations in the far north; they can be dangerous because of extreme cold.

8. What do readers learn about the far north from "Come to Alaska" that will help them better understand "To Build a Fire"?
   A. Alaska has a number of active volcanoes.
   B. The *average* winter temperature in Alaska is -11° F.
   C. Alaska has the 16 highest mountain peaks in North America.
   D. During the summer in Alaska, the sun shines about 20 hours a day.

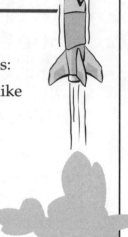

Reading Across Genres
Lesson 12 Summary

When reading across genres, remember the following tips:

- Determine how the main ideas of the passages are alike or different.

- Compare details in the two passages.

- Compare the purposesw of the two passages.

- Use one passage to help you understand the other.

Practice Passages

Directions: Read both passages, then answer the questions that follow.

Passage 1:

Life on Mars?
by Conrad Mencken

1   For centuries, humans have imagined life in other parts of the universe. Science-fiction writers and filmmakers have given us all kinds of stories in which humans travel into space and have adventures with <u>aliens</u>. Other times, those aliens visit us and either try to be our friends or try to harm us. The planet Mars is our closest neighbor, and this red planet has long fascinated humans, who have often asked themselves, "Could there be life on Mars?"

2   In July 1976, NASA landed two space probes on Mars. What they found did not answer the question, but it did give evidence offering possibilities. Though the *Viking* space probes found no clear sign of life, they did find dry river beds, inactive volcanoes, and a harsh environment where life just might have existed long, long ago.

3   Then, in August 1996, a startling announcement was made by President Clinton at the White House. The president's information was later explained with great detail in the August 16 issue of *Science* magazine. Scientists were now convinced that a meteorite found in

Antarctica had come from Mars. When scientists studied the meteorite, they found features of possible fossils, indicating that many years ago—well over a billion—life could have existed on Mars. (How did scientists determine that the meteorite came from Mars? They compared it to Martian samples studied by the *Viking* space probes.)

Viking 2 on a Martian plain.

4   It may take many years to prove conclusively that life once existed on Mars. Perhaps we will never know. But, until the question has been fully answered, one thing remains certain: It will continue to be asked. ❖

Passage 2:

The War of the Worlds *was published in 1898. In the book, the author imagines an invasion by people from Mars. Here is a part of that story.*

adapted by Alan Noble from

The War of the Worlds

by H. G. Wells

1   Then came the night of the first falling star. It was seen early in the morning, rushing eastward over the town of Winchester, a line of flame high in the atmosphere. Hundreds must have seen it and taken it for an ordinary falling star. Some described it as leaving a greenish streak behind it that glowed for some seconds.

2   Very early in the morning, my friend Ogilvey, who had seen the shooting star and who thought that a meteorite should lay somewhere on the common,[1] took off to find it. Find it he did, soon after dawn, and not far from the sand pits. The Thing itself lay almost entirely buried in sand, amid the scattered splinters of a fir tree it had split into fragments during its fiery landing.

3   Ogilvey was all alone on the common. He stood at the edge of the hole the Thing had made for itself, staring at its strange appearance, surprised mostly by its unusual shape and color. The only sounds it made were faint movements from within the cylinder.

[1] **common:** a plot of land for everybody's use, as a common pasture

4   Then he noticed that, very slowly, the circular top of the cylinder was rotating on its body. It was such a gradual movement that he discovered it only through noticing that a black mark that had been near him five minutes ago was now at the other side of the circumference. Even then he scarcely understood what this meant, until he heard a muffled grating sound and saw the black mark jerk forward an inch or so. Then he understood in a flash. The cylinder was artificial—hollow— with an end that screwed out! Something within the cylinder was unscrewing the top!

Earth as seen from outer space.

5   "Good heavens!" he said. "There's a man in it—men in it! Half roasted to death! Trying to escape!"

6   At once, with a quick mental leap, he linked the Thing with the flashes that people had been recently seeing on the surface of Mars.

7   The thought of the confined creatures was so dreadful to him that he forgot the heat and went forward to the cylinder to help turn. But luckily the dull radiation stopped him before he could burn his hands on the still-glowing metal. With that, Ogilvey stood for a moment not knowing what to do, then he turned, scrambled out of the pit, and set off running wildly toward the town of Woking. ❖

Sample Genre Questions

1. Which of the following best tells the purpose of Passage 1?
   A. to persuade the government to continue Mars research
   B. to describe the flight and landing of the Viking space probes
   C. to inform the reader of recent research concerning life on Mars
   D. to explain why science-fiction writers often write about alien visits

2. Which of the following best tells the purpose of Passage 2?
   A. to persuade the reader to believe in men from Mars
   B. to describe the Martian invaders and their weapons
   C. to inform the reader of recent research concerning life on Mars
   D. to entertain the reader with a science-fiction story about a visit from Mars

3. Which of the following is one way the two passages are similar?
   A. Both selections are nonfiction.
   B. Both selections discuss scientific study.
   C. Both selections describe cylinders falling from the sky.
   D. Both selections deal with Mars and Martian life forms.

4. In which way are the two passages different?
   A. One is fiction about Mars; the other is science fiction about Mars.
   B. One is about Earth sending spacecraft to Mars; the other is about Mars sending spacecraft to Earth.
   C. One tells about Earth sending people to Mars; the other tells about Venus sending people to Mars.
   D. One tells why scientists believe life could have lived on Mars; the other tells why life could not survive there.

5. How does the author of Passage 1 organize his material?
   A. by presenting problems and their solutions
   B. by covering most important information to least important information
   C. by covering least important information to most important information
   D. by giving one point with its supporting details, then going to the next point with its supporting details, and so on

6. How does the author of Passage 2 organize his material?

   A. by discussing events in the order that those events occur

   B. by covering most important information to least important information

   C. by covering least important information to most important information

   D. by giving one point with its supporting details, then going to the next point with its supporting details, and so on

7. Based on the passages, both writers would probably agree that

   A. Mars is an interesting planet.

   B. the Earth is in danger of an attack from Mars.

   C. most falling stars are actually spacemen from the planet Mars.

   D. science will never find out if there is (or has been) life on Mars.

8. Look at this chart comparing the two passages.

Story Differences

Life on Mars	The War of the Worlds
• Earth sends space probes to Mars	• Mars sends space probes to Earth
• Earth's space probes carry no humans	• Mars' space probes do carry Martians
• Life on Mars could have existed billions of years ago	• _____

Which of the following best completes the chart?

A. Life on Mars is very primitive.

B. Two U.S. space probes land on Mars.

C. Life on Mars *does* exist in modern times.

D. Creatures on Mars live in metal cylinders.

Additional Practice Questions

9. According to Passage 1, NASA first landed two *Viking* space probes on Mars in
   A. 1967.
   B. 1969.
   C. 1976.
   D. 1989.

10. In Passage 1, paragraph 1, what does the word *aliens* mean?
    A. people from another planet
    B. people who work for NASA
    C. people from another country
    D. people who act in science-fiction movies

11. In Passage 2, which word best describes the character of Ogilvey?
    A. curious
    B. mean
    C. shy
    D. dangerous

12. Give two examples of how the author's choice of words in *The War of the Worlds* appeals to the readers' senses.

    _____

    _____

    _____

    _____

    _____

Lesson 13

Information at a Glance

Reference materials and factual articles sometimes contain information arranged in special ways. Informational reading often includes the following:

- Charts and Tables
- Graphs
- Maps
- Diagrams

These information displays are called **graphics**. Graphics are not difficult to read once you understand how they are organized. This lesson will review the kinds of graphics that you are most likely to find on a reading test.

Tip 1 **Charts and tables display facts so they can be compared and understood at a glance.**

Each box of information on a chart or table is called a **cell**. A cell is usually named by its **column** and **row**. For example, in the table on page 167, the cell in Row 2, Column 2, identifies the number of comedies (720) rented at Front Row Video in the month of February.

NOTE: The terms row and column refer ONLY to boxes containing information that changes. **Title boxes**, such as the table title (Front Row Video: Video Rentals by Category), and **label boxes** (New Release, Comedy, January, February, etc.), are NOT considered rows or columns. DO NOT count them when looking for a particular cell in a table.

To read a chart or table, follow these steps:

- Check the **title** to find out what type of information is being presented.
- Read the **labels** to find out what the columns and rows represent.
- Examine the **question** to determine what specific information you need to find.

Practice Activity 1

Mr. Jenkins is the manager of Front Row Video. He wants to make a table that shows how many videotapes (by type) have been rented during the months of January through April. This is the table he prepared.

Front Row Video
Video Rentals by Category (Year to Date)

	January	February	March	April
New Release	1,792	1,533	1,615	1,399
Comedy	542	720	465	394
Drama	422	398	512	287
Action-Adventure	695	521	443	312

Directions: Use the table to answer the following questions.

1. What kind of information can Mr. Jenkins get from this table?
   A. the total number of videos sold at his store during the year
   B. the types of videos available at his store during a four-month period
   C. the number of customers visiting his store during a four-month period
   D. the number of videos rented (by type) at his store during a four-month period

2. What number did Mr. Jenkins put in Row 3, Column 4?
   A. 394
   B. 287
   C. 443
   D. 512

3. If Mr. Jenkins wanted to add rental information for the month of May, what would he have to add to the table?
   A. a new table title
   B. another information row with "May" label
   C. another information column with "May" label
   D. another information row and new table title

4. Which type of video did Mr. Jenkins rent least in March?
   A. New Release
   B. Comedy
   C. Drama
   D. Action-Adventure

5. How many comedies did Mr. Jenkins rent in January?
   A. 422
   B. 542
   C. 720
   D. 1,792

Tip 2 **Circle graphs show parts that add up to a whole.**

A **circle graph**, or **pie chart**, is a graph in the shape of a circle. The circle represents 100 percent, or a whole. Each piece of the circle represents a part (or percentage) of the whole. Bigger slices represent bigger parts of the whole, and smaller slices represent smaller parts. The pieces always add up to 100 percent.

To read a circle graph, follow these steps:

- Check the **title** to find out what the whole graph represents.

- Read the **labels** to find out what each slice represents.

- Compare the **slices** to get an overall picture of the information.

- Examine the **question** to make sure you know what you're looking for.

Practice Activity 2

Mrs. Cohen's social studies class took a survey to see how students spend their own money. After the students collected their data, they made a circle graph to show how the class, as a whole, spent its money. Here is what their pie chart looked like.

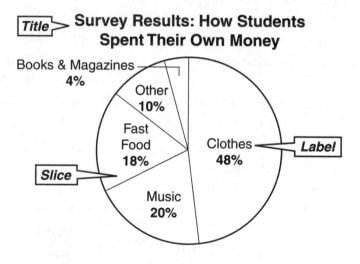

Directions: Use the pie chart to answer the following questions.

6. Mrs. Cohen's students spent the least amount of their money on which of the following?

   A. books and magazines

   B. other items

   C. clothes

   D. food

7. Mrs. Cohen's students spent about half of their money on

   A. food.

   B. clothes.

   C. music.

   D. other items.

Tip 3 **Bar graphs compare related things.**

The process of reading bar and line graphs is very similar to reading circle graphs. To read a bar graph, follow these steps:

- Read the **title** to make sure you understand what kind of information is being presented.

- Read the **labels** on each axis.

- Compare the **bars** to get an overall picture of the information.

- Examine the **question** to make sure you understand what you're looking for in the graph.

The amount being measured in a graph is usually described on one side (**axis**) of the graph. The kind of information being measured is usually described along the bottom of the graph. Be sure you understand what is being measured and what kind of measuring unit is being used.

Most bar graphs will show **units** measured on one axis (as in number of students) and a **variable** (the thing being measured) on the other (as in type of transportation). Bar graphs usually compare related things.

By adding together the number of items measured on each bar, you can find the total number of items being compared.

Look at the sample bar graph that follows. It shows how 16 students in Mrs. Chong's class travel to school on most days.

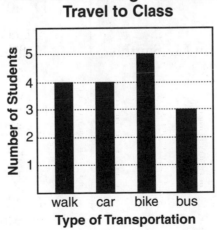

The vertical (up and down) axis shows the number of students (1 through 5), and the horizontal (left to right) axis shows the kinds of transportation used.

This bar graph shows that 4 students walk, 4 students come by car, 5 students ride their bikes, and 3 students take the bus.

Practice Activity 3

Students in Mr. Smith's science class wanted to know the eye color of their classmates. After collecting their data, they made this bar graph.

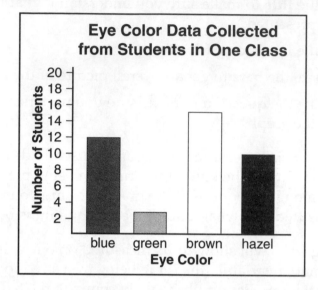

Directions: Use the students' bar graph to answer the following questions.

8. Which eye color is most common among Mr. Smith's students?

   A. blue

   B. green

   C. brown

   D. hazel

9. How many students in Mr. Smith's class have blue eyes?

   A. 10

   B. 12

   C. 14

   D. 16

10. How many students were surveyed altogether?

    A. 4

    B. 15

    C. 20

    D. 40

11. If three more students with brown eyes joined the class, which of the following changes would have to be made to the graph?

    A. The "brown" color bar would need to be increased by three.

    B. The title of the bar graph would have to be changed.

    C. A new bar would have to be added to the graph.

    D. The "Eye Color" axis would need more color bars.

> *Tip 4* **Line graphs show changes over time.**
>
> Line graphs show the relationship between two variables, including changes and trends over time. To read a line graph, follow these steps:
>
> • Read the **title** to make sure you understand what kind of information is being presented.
>
> • Read the **labels** on each axis.
>
> • Compare the **points** that are connected by the line to get an overall picture of the information.
>
> • Examine the **question** to make sure you understand what you're looking for in the graph.

Practice Activity 4

The cafeteria manager at Martin Luther King Jr. Middle School needed to order supplies for a new school year. To help him in his planning, he made a line graph and plotted the average number of students per day who ate lunch in the cafeteria the previous year. Here is the cafeteria manager's graph.

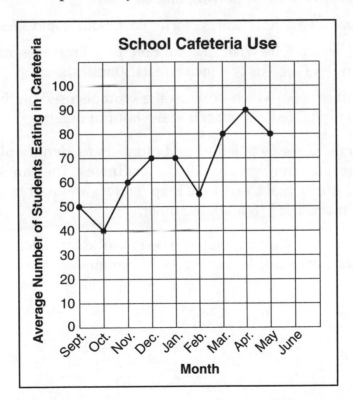

Directions: Use the line graph to answer the following questions.

12. During which month did the most students use the school cafeteria?

    A. December   C. April

    B. January   D. May

13. During which of the following periods did cafeteria use increase most?

    A. September to October

    B. October to November

    C. February to March

    D. March to April

14. According to the line graph, about how many students per day should the cafeteria manager plan to serve during the month of September?

    A. 40

    B. 50

    C. 70

    D. 90

Tip 5 **Maps show direction, distance, natural features (such as lakes and rivers), and human-made features (such as roads and towns).**

Most maps provide the following guides:

- a **compass**, which indicates North, East, South, and West.

- a **scale**, which tells what each unit on the map represents in terms of actual miles (such as one inch equals 50 miles).

- a **legend** or **key**, which explains the symbols used on the map. Legends are usually boxed and placed at the bottom of a map.

Maps often use a series of letters and numbers to identify places on the map. These letters and numbers are called **coordinates**. They are shown along the vertical and horizontal axes of the map. Letters are used to mark one axis, and numbers are used to mark the other.

Any place on the following map can be identified by a letter and number combination. For example, the Spruce Mountain Resort is at F2.

Practice Activity 5

Angie Maldonado and her family are on a one-week camping trip in the mountains around Mosquito Flats. Her father has used a road atlas to find the town of Mosquito Flats.

Directions: Use this page from Mr. Maldonado's atlas to answer the questions that follow.

15. What kind of road would the Maldonado family take to drive from Mosquito Flats to Peaceful Lake?

   A. an interstate highway

   B. a U.S. highway

   C. a state highway

   D. a state secondary road

16. According to Mr. Maldonado's map, the distance by road between Mosquito Flats and Metropolis is about how many miles?

   A. 20

   B. 40

   C. 90

   D. 150

17. If Mr. Maldonado wanted to find Sweetwater on the map, at which coordinates should he look?

   A. H2

   B. H1

   C. G2

   D. G1

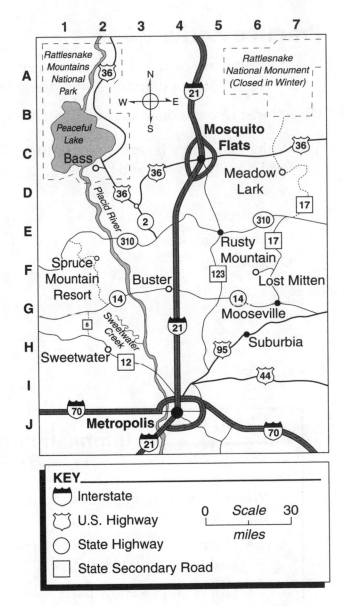

18. If the Maldonado family drove from Mooseville to Buster on State Highway 14, in what general direction would they be heading?

   A. north

   B. south

   C. east

   D. west

Tip 6 **Diagrams show relationships.**

A diagram shows how something is made, how it works, or how the parts are related to each other. A diagram can very quickly show something that might take several paragraphs to explain. (See page 100 in Lesson 8 for an example.) Whenever you see a diagram, look carefully at any labels or arrows.

Practice Activity 6

Earth is made up of three main parts, or layers: the crust, mantle, and core. The following diagram shows these layers.

Directions: Use the diagram to answer the question that follows.

19. Which of Earth's layers is part of the land on which we stand?

   A. crust

   B. mantle

   C. outer core

   D. inner core

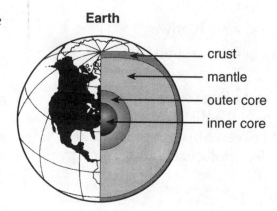

Earth

crust
mantle
outer core
inner core

Information at a Glance

Lesson 13 Summary

When answering questions about graphics, remember the following tips:

- Charts and tables display facts so they can be compared and understood at a glance.

- Circle graphs show parts that add up to a whole.

- Bar graphs compare related things.

- Line graphs show changes over time.

- Maps show direction, distance, natural features (such as lakes and rivers), and human-made features (such as roads and towns).

- Diagrams show relationships.

Sample Visual Information Questions

Directions: Look at the map, read the paragraph from a report about the Bermuda Triangle, and answer Numbers 1 through 3.

The Bermuda Triangle

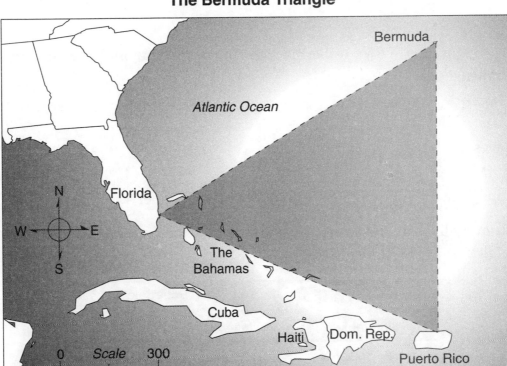

Although the boundaries of the Bermuda Triangle have been disputed, most people agree on a triangle with tips touching the Bermuda Islands, the coast of the United States, and Puerto Rico.

Some scientists believe strange weather phenomena,[1] such as violent storms or downward air currents, destroyed the many ships and planes that have mysteriously disappeared in the Bermuda Triangle. Fast-moving ocean currents may then have swept the remains of the ships and planes far from where they first disappeared.

[1] **phenomena:** extraordinary events

1. What do the map and its caption tell you that the report does not?

_____

_____

_____

_____

2. Each side of the Bermuda Triangle is about how long?

    A. 300 miles

    B. 1,000 miles

    C. 2,000 miles

    D. 5,000 miles

3. To get from Puerto Rico to Bermuda, a ship or plane would have to travel

    A. north.

    B. south.

    C. east.

    D. west.

Directions: Use the following schedule to answer Number 4.

Tommy lives in New York. He wants to take the *Capitol Special* to visit his cousin Brian in Philadelphia.

Timetable	Train Schedule	
	Capitol Special	*Virginia Flyer*
leave New York, NY	11:10 A.M.	12:40 P.M.
arrive Philadelphia, PA	12:30 P.M.	2:05 P.M.
leave Philadelphia, PA	12:40 P.M.	2:15 P.M.
arrive Washington, D.C.	3:10 P.M.	4:45 P.M.
leave Washington, D.C.	3:40 P.M.	5:10 P.M.
arrive Richmond, VA	5:10 P.M.	6:30 P.M.

4. According to the schedule, if Tommy leaves New York at 11:10 A.M., what time will he arrive in Philadelphia?

    A. 12:30 P.M.

    B. 12:40 P.M.

    C. 2:05 P.M.

    D. 2:15 P.M.

Directions: Use the following graph to answer Numbers 5 and 6.

The students in Mr. Lindstrom's music classes did a survey to compare the types of music students liked best. They sampled 100 students from four classes. Each student was allowed to vote only once. The results are shown in the graph below.

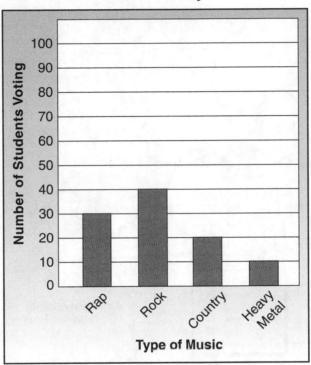

Music Survey

5. According to the graph, students preferred

    A. rap over rock.

    B. country over rap.

    C. country over rock.

    D. country over heavy metal.

6. Which circle graph best displays the students' data?

    A.

    B.
    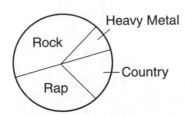

    C.
    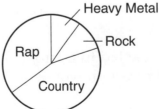

    D.

Directions: Use the following map to answer Numbers 7 through 13.

Bob will begin work tomorrow as a Park Ranger at Yellowstone National Park. Today he is studying a map of the park to become familiar with its layout.

Yellowstone National Park

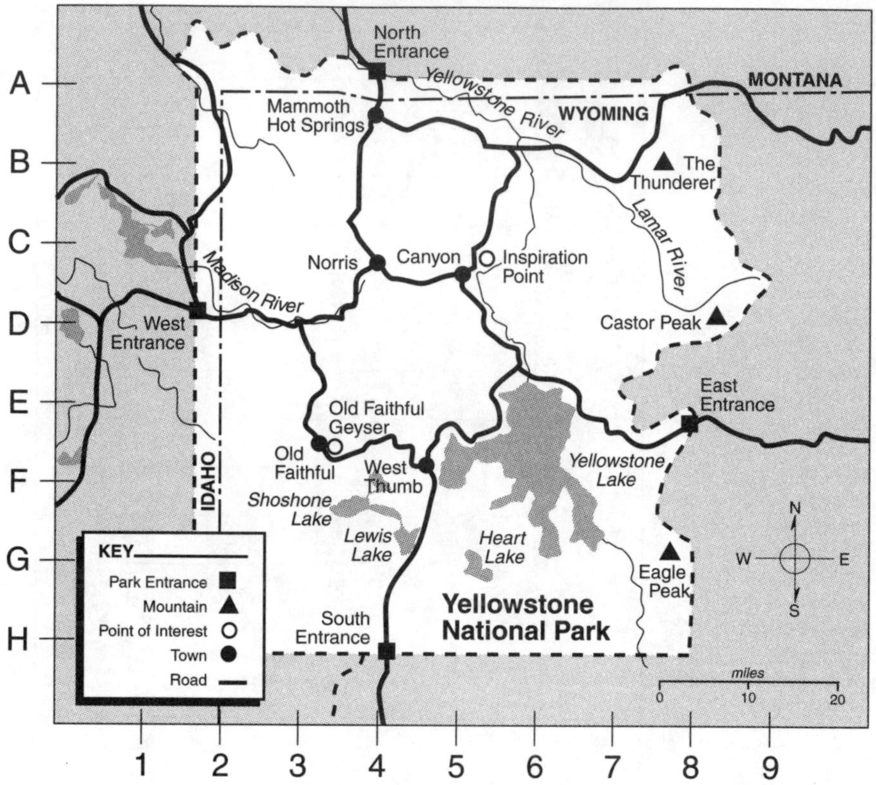

7. Ranger Bob will find the South Entrance to Yellowstone Park located at

   A. A4.

   B. E8.

   C. D2.

   D. H4.

8. If Ranger Bob wanted to go from Old Faithful to Mammoth Hot Springs, in which general direction would he need to travel?

   A. east

   B. west

   C. north

   D. south

9. Which of the following locations would Ranger Bob find farthest east on the map?

    A. Norris

    B. Canyon

    C. Castor Peak

    D. Inspiration Point

10. Using the map, Ranger Bob would find that the distance from the South Entrance to West Thumb is approximately

    A. 5 miles.

    B. 20 miles.

    C. 40 miles.

    D. 50 miles.

11. Using the map's key, Ranger Bob would find that The Thunderer is a

    A. town.

    B. mountain.

    C. park entrance.

    D. point of interest.

12. Which point of interest is closest to the town of Canyon?

    A. Eagle Peak

    B. West Thumb

    C. Inspiration Point

    D. Old Faithful Guyser

13. Which park entrance is closest to Mammoth Hot Springs?

    A. North Entrance

    B. East Entrance

    C. South Entrance

    D. West Entrance

Appendix

◆ *Ohio Academic Content Standards and Benchmarks for English Language Arts: Reading, Grade 5*

◆ *Ohio Proficiency Learning Outcomes for Reading, Grade 5*

Ohio Academic Content Standards and Benchmarks for English Language Arts: Reading, Grade 5

Blast Off on Ohio Reading, Level 5, is based on the Ohio Academic Content Standards and Grades 4–7 Benchmarks for Reading using the Grade 5 Indicators as a guideline for specific skill coverage. The following table matches the benchmarks and indicators to the *Blast Off* lessons in which they are addressed. Asterisks (*) indicate benchmark skills found in Grade 4, 6, or 7 Indicators.

ACQUISITION OF VOCABULARY STANDARD	*Blast Off* Lesson(s)
Students acquire vocabulary through exposure to language-rich situations, such as reading books and other texts and conversing with adults and peers. They use context clues, as well as direct explanations provided by others, to gain new words. They learn to apply word analysis skills to build and extend their own vocabulary. As students progress through the grades, they become more proficient in applying their knowledge of words (origins, parts, relationships, meanings) to acquire specialized vocabulary that aids comprehension.	
GRADES 4–7 BENCHMARKS	
A. Use context clues and text structures to determine the meaning of new vocabulary.	3
B. Infer word meaning through identification and analysis of analogies* and other word relationships.	3
C. Apply knowledge of connotation and denotation to learn the meanings of words.	3
D. Use knowledge of symbols*, acronyms*, word origins and derivations to determine the meanings of unknown words.	4
E. Use knowledge of roots and affixes to determine the meanings of complex words.	4
F. Use multiple resources to enhance comprehension of vocabulary.	4
GRADE 5 INDICATORS: ACQUISITION OF VOCABULARY	
Contextual Understanding	
1. Define the meaning of unknown words by using context clues and the author's use of definition, restatement and example.	3
2. Use context clues to determine the meaning of synonyms, antonyms, homophones, homonyms and homographs.	3
Conceptual Understanding	
3. Identify the connotation and denotation of new words.	3
4. Identify and understand new uses of words and phrases in text, such as similes and metaphors.	3, 7
Structural Understanding	
5. Use word origins to determine the meaning of unknown words and phrases.	4
6. Apply the knowledge of prefixes, suffixes and roots and their various inflections to analyze the meanings of words.	4
7. Identify the meanings of abbreviations.	4
Tools and Resources	
8. Determine the meanings and pronunciations of unknown words by using dictionaries, thesauruses, glossaries, technology and textual features, such as definitional footnotes or sidebars.	4

READING PROCESS: CONCEPTS OF PRINT, COMPREHENSION STRATEGIES AND SELF-MONITORING STRATEGIES STANDARD	*Blast Off* Lesson(s)
Students develop and learn to apply strategies that help them to comprehend and interpret informational and literary texts. Reading and learning to read are problem-solving processes that require strategies for the reader to make sense of written language and remain engaged with texts. Beginners develop basic concepts about print (e.g., that print holds meaning) and how books work (e.g., text organization). As strategic readers, students learn to analyze and evaluate texts to demonstrate their understanding of text. Additionally, students learn to self-monitor their own comprehension by asking and answering questions about the text, self-correcting errors and assessing their own understanding. They apply these strategies effectively to assigned and self-selected texts read in and out of the classroom.	

GRADES 4–7 BENCHMARKS

A. Determine a purpose for reading and use a range of reading comprehension strategies to better understand text.	5
B. Apply effective reading comprehension strategies, including summarizing and making predictions and comparisons, using information in text, between text and across subject areas.	All Lessons
C. Make meaning through asking and responding to a variety of questions related to text.	All Lessons
D. Apply self-monitoring strategies to clarify confusion about text and to monitor comprehension.	5

GRADE 5 INDICATORS: READING PROCESS: CONCEPTS OF PRINT, COMPREHENSION STRATEGIES AND SELF-MONITORING STRATEGIES

Comprehension Strategies

1. Establish and adjust purposes for reading, including to find out, to understand, to interpret, to enjoy and to solve problems.	5
2. Predict and support predictions with specific references to textual examples that may be in widely separated sections of text.	5, 6, 9
3. Make critical comparisons across texts.	11, 12
4. Summarize the information in texts, recognizing that there may be several important ideas rather than just one main idea and identifying details that support each.	1, 2, 5
5. Make inferences based on implicit information in texts, and provide justifications for those inferences.	6, 9
6. Select, create and use graphic organizers to interpret textual information.	5, 6, 9
7. Answer literal, inferential and evaluative questions to demonstrate comprehension of grade-appropriate print texts and electronic and visual media.	All Lessons

Self-Monitoring Strategies

8. Monitor own comprehension by adjusting speed to fit the purpose, or by skimming, scanning, reading on, looking back or summarizing what has been read so far in text.	5
9. List questions and search for answers within the text to construct meaning.	5

Independent Reading

10. Use criteria to choose independent reading materials (e.g., personal interest, knowledge of authors and genres or recommendations from others).	5, Indep. Activity
11. Independently read books for various purposes (e.g., for enjoyment, for literary experience, to gain information or to perform a task).	5, Indep. Activity

READING APPLICATIONS: INFORMATIONAL, TECHNICAL AND PERSUASIVE TEXT STANDARD	*Blast Off* Lesson(s)
Students gain information from reading for the purposes of learning about a subject, doing a job, making decisions and accomplishing a task. Students need to apply the reading process to various types of informational texts, including essays, magazines, newspapers, textbooks, instruction manuals, consumer and workplace documents, reference materials, multimedia and electronic resources. They learn to attend to text features, such as titles, subtitles and visual aids, to make predictions and build text knowledge. They learn to read diagrams, charts, graphs, maps and displays in text as sources of additional information. Students use their knowledge of text structure to organize content information, analyze it and draw inferences from it. Strategic readers learn to recognize arguments, bias, stereotyping and propaganda in informational text sources.	

GRADES 4–7 BENCHMARKS

A.	Use text features and graphics to organize, analyze and draw inferences from content and to gain additional information.	5, 8, 13
B.	Recognize the difference between cause and effect and fact and opinion to analyze text.	8, 9, 10
C.	Explain how main ideas connect to each other in a variety of sources.	8, 11, 12
D.	Identify arguments and persuasive techniques used in informational text.	10
E.	Explain the treatment, scope and organization of ideas from different texts to draw conclusions about a topic.	8, 11, 12
F.	Determine the extent to which a summary accurately reflects the main idea, critical details and underlying meaning of original text.	1, 2

GRADE 5 INDICATORS: READING APPLICATIONS: INFORMATIONAL, TECHNICAL AND PERSUASIVE TEXT

1.	Use text features, such as chapter titles, headings and subheadings; parts of books including the index and table of contents and online tools (search engines) to locate information.	5, 8
2.	Identify, distinguish between and explain examples of cause and effect in informational text.	8, 9
3.	Compare important details about a topic, using different sources of information, including books, magazines, newspapers and online resources.	8, 11
4.	Summarize the main ideas and supporting details.	1, 2, 5, 8
5.	Analyze information found in maps, charts, tables, graphs and diagrams.	8, 13
6.	Clarify steps in a set of instructions or procedures for proper sequencing and completeness and revise if necessary.	8
7.	Analyze the difference between fact and opinion.	10
8.	Distinguish relevant from irrelevant information in a text and identify possible points of confusion for the reader.	8
9.	Identify and understand an author's purpose for writing, including to explain, to entertain or to inform.	8, 10, 11

READING APPLICATIONS: LITERARY TEXT STANDARD	*Blast Off* Lesson(s)
Students enhance their understanding of the human story by reading literary texts that represent a variety of authors, cultures and eras. They learn to apply the reading process to the various genres of literature, including fables, tales, short stories, novels, poetry and drama. They demonstrate their comprehension by describing and discussing the elements of literature (e.g., setting, character and plot), analyzing the author's use of language (e.g., word choice and figurative language), comparing and contrasting texts, inferring theme and meaning and responding to text in critical and creative ways. Strategic readers learn to explain, analyze and critique literary text to achieve deep understanding.	

GRADES 4–7 BENCHMARKS

A.	Describe and analyze the elements of character development.	6
B.	Analyze the importance of setting.	6
C.	Identify the elements of plot and establish a connection between an element and a future event.	1, 6, 9
D.	Differentiate between the points of view in narrative text.	6
E.	Demonstrate comprehension by inferring themes, patterns* and symbols*.	1, 7, 12
F.	Identify similarities and differences of various literary forms and genres.	5, 6, 7, 8, 12
G.	Explain how figurative language expresses ideas and conveys mood.	6, 7

GRADE 5 INDICATORS: READING APPLICATIONS: LITERARY TEXT

1.	Explain how a character's thoughts, words and actions reveal his or her motivations.	6
2.	Explain the influence of setting on the selection.	6
3.	Identify the main incidents of a plot sequence and explain how they influence future action.	1, 6, 9
4.	Identify the speaker and explain how point of view affects the text.	6
5.	Summarize stated and implied themes.	1, 7, 12
6.	Describe the defining characteristics of literary forms and genres, including poetry, drama, chapter books, biographies, fiction and non-fiction.	5, 6, 7, 8, 12
7.	Interpret how an author's choice of words appeals to the senses and suggests mood.	6, 7
8.	Identify and explain the use of figurative language in literary works, including idioms, similes, hyperboles, metaphors and personification.	3, 7

Ohio Proficiency Learning Outcomes for Reading, Grade 5

Blast Off on Ohio Reading, Level 5, has also been matched to the following sixth-grade proficiency learning outcomes to help with instructional planning during Ohio's transitional testing phase.

OUTCOMES	*Blast Off* Lesson(s)
Strand I – Constructing/Examining Meaning with Fiction Selections **Given a fiction or poetry text to read silently, learners will demonstrate an understanding of text and elements of fiction or poetry by responding to items in which they:**	
1. Analyze aspects of the text, examining, for example, characters, setting, plot, problem/solution, point of view, or theme.	1, 6, 9
2. Summarize the text.	1, 2, 5
3. Infer from the text.	3, 6, 9
4. Respond to the text.	All Lessons
Strand II – Extending Meaning with Fiction Selections **Given a fiction or poetry text to read silently, learners will demonstrate an understanding of text and elements of fiction or poetry by responding to items in which they:**	
5. Compare and contrast aspects of the text, for example, characters or settings.	6, 9
6. Critique and evaluate the text.	6, 7
7. Select information for a variety of purposes, including enjoyment.	5
8. Express reasons for recommending or not recommending the text for a particular audience or purpose.	5
9. Explain how an author uses contents of a text to support his/her purpose for writing.	10
Strand III – Constructing/Examining Meaning with Nonfiction Selections **Given a nonfiction text to read silently, learners will demonstrate an understanding of text and elements of nonfiction by responding to items in which they:**	
10. Analyze the text, examining, for example, author's use of comparison and contrast, cause and effect, or fact and opinion.	8, 9, 10
11. Summarize the text.	1, 2, 5
12. Infer from the text.	3, 9
13. Respond to the text.	All Lessons
Strand IV – Extending Meaning with Nonfiction Selections **Given a nonfiction text to read silently, learners will demonstrate an understanding of text and elements of nonfiction by responding to items in which they:**	
14. Compare and/or contrast aspects of the text.	9, 11
15. Critique and evaluate the text for such elements as organizational structure and logical reasoning.	8
16. Select information from a variety of resources to support ideas, concepts, and interpretations.	8
17. Express reasons for recommending or not recommending the text for a particular audience or purpose.	5
18. Explain how an author uses contents of a text to support his/her purpose for writing.	10